ADRIAN WALLWORK

BUSINESS
OPTIONS

TEACHER'S BOOK

OXFORD
UNIVERSITY PRESS

Oxford University Press, Great Clarendon Street, Oxford
OX2 6DP

Oxford New York
Athens Auckland Bangkok Bogotá
Buenos Aires Calcutta Cape Town Chennai
Dar es Salaam Delhi Florence Hong Kong
Istanbul Karachi Kuala Lumpur Madrid
Melbourne Mexico City Mumbai Nairobi
Paris São Paulo Singapore Taipei Tokyo
Toronto Warsaw

and associated companies in
Berlin Ibadan

OXFORD and OXFORD ENGLISH
are trade marks of Oxford University Press

ISBN 0 19 457235 8

Photocopying

Typeset by Oxford University Press

Printed in China

Acknowledgements
The authors and publisher are grateful to those who have
given permission to reproduce extracts and adaptations of
copyright material. Although every effort has been made
to trace and contact copyright holders before publication,
this has not always been possible. We apologize for any
apparent infringement of copyright and if notified, the
publisher will be pleased to rectify any errors or omissions
at the earliest opportunity.

p 28 Lamalle Report on Top Executives of the 1990s,
quoted in David Peoples, *Presentations Plus*, John Wylie &
Sons Inc.
pp 41 and 75 *Life-Spans: Or How Long Things Last* by Frank
Kendig and Richard Hulton. Holt, Rinehart & Winston.
p 48 *Do's & Taboos of Hosting International Visitors* by Roger
Axtell. Copyright © Roger Axtell 1990. Reprinted by
permission of John Wiley & Sons, Inc.

With thanks to Anne Watson for her contribution to the
manuscript.

CONTENTS

Introduction   5

1   **Protocol**   8

2   **Meetings**   13

3   **Organization**   18

4   **Numbers**   13

5   **Communication**   28

6   **Travel**   33

7   **Planning**   37

8   **Products**   41

9   **Visiting**   46

10 **Entertaining**   51

11 **Presentations**   56

12 **Performance**   61

13 **Negotiating**   66

14 **Trade**   70

Photocopiable activities   74

Progress tests   76

Answer key to tests   93

INTRODUCTION

AIMS AND LEVEL

Business Options is suitable for professional people from all areas of business. Although aimed principally at those with business experience, most of the tasks are also suitable for students following courses in business subjects which include English as part of the curriculum. Activities are provided which are suitable for in-company groups whose participants often have very specific needs, and open groups, which are likely to be less homogeneous. This Teacher's Book provides alternative activities for monolingual and multilingual groups where appropriate; many of these are in the *Warm-up* section which begins each unit.

'Business English' is intended to mean *all* the language needed to do business effectively, i.e. not only the language required in the workplace (for meetings, telephone calls, describing processes, etc.), but also the survival skills needed for travelling abroad and the socializing skills needed around a lunch or dinner table.

Working people generally tend to be pushed for time and need to exploit their English lessons to the full. The Student's Book therefore focuses mainly on oral communication skills, with listening and reading as input for speaking activities. Writing tasks are mainly tackled in the Workbook, as students tend to carry out these tasks outside class time and without the aid of a teacher.

The book is based on these main premises:

– teachers may be unfamiliar with some areas of business covered in the book, and so explanations of business theory and practice are provided in the teacher's notes

– students should be able to see how the language of their everyday lives can also be applied to the business world (for example, negotiating an increase in pocket money with your child can involve using the same kind of persuading language as negotiating a price rise for your product with a customer)

– students at this level will have met most language structures before, and so the approach to grammar is inductive and analytical; learning styles vary, however, and the Reference section in the Student's Book includes a comprehensive presentation of those grammar points covered in the units

– students should be given the opportunity to learn how business works in all parts of the world; there is therefore a strong cross-cultural input, though the models themselves are generally based on business practice in the UK and the USA.

RESEARCH

My aim while writing this book was to put myself in the student's shoes as much as possible to discover the type of problems they might have. For example, to understand what kind of questions students might want to ask or be asked while visiting a factory, I visited the Ford plant at Dagenham (UK). To learn presentations skills I went to watch various experts in the field, for example Don Daughters, the Worldwide Manager of IBM, whom I then interviewed about his techniques. With some of my own clients I gained practical experience in how to run meetings, organize congresses and trade fairs, and set up websites. To get some tips on negotiation I contacted an expert from Frosch Learning, a group of management consultants. The interviews were then re-recorded, so that what students will hear on the audio cassettes is authentic language presented with the clarity provided by the recording studio. The reading materials are also all authentic and come from a variety of sources (see *Business skills* below).

STRUCTURE

The book has 14 theme-based units which follow a logical progression from unit 1, *Protocol*, where students get to know each other and learn about customs connected with business protocol around the world. In other units students learn how to make contact with potential clients, travel and visit clients, talk about their products and services, present them formally, negotiate deals, and finally market their products at trade fairs. Each unit is self-standing, however, and if, for example, your students are going to have to give a presentation in the near future, you could go directly to unit 11, *Presentations*.

Within each unit the structure is as follows:

Did you know?

This consists of ten facts and figures (occasionally quotations too) related to the theme of the unit, which concern both strictly business statistics and also information of general interest. These provide an introduction to the unit through the kind of information that students might read in everyday life. The statistics come mainly from the business press and from books and articles written by management specialists.

Students can read these facts for interest, as a warm-up to the unit, or use them as the basis for a lesson. Suggestions are given in the teacher's notes to each unit.

Language Work

This begins with a sub-section on speech production, and covers stress (word and sentence), intonation, and pronunciation. I interviewed both native and non-native speakers to find out the problems they had with understanding each other. It seemed that the main barrier to communication was mispronunciation and applying the wrong stress pattern. It is beyond the scope of a general business English course to go into detail on the difficulties encountered by speakers of particular host languages; the focus here is on encouraging students to sound natural and confident, and to regard this as being as important as using the correct vocabulary and structures.

The language presented in each unit is appropriate to the unit theme. Reported speech is covered in unit 5, *Communication*, for example, and passives in unit 8, *Products*. Grammar is presented through concept-checking questions which invite students to analyse the language, and there is also a detailed Reference section at the back of the Student's Book. There is a short practice exercise in the Student's Book, and more extensive practice in the Workbook.

This section also introduces key vocabulary and phrases through the reading and listening passages, which are used to contextualize the language work and prepare for the skills work which follows.

Business Skills

Students are now given the opportunity to practise the language and structures learned in the previous section in a freer context. This section also contains a short authentic reading exercise. The texts are not primarily aimed at comprehension, though there is some vocabulary work, but more as a springboard to discussion through cross-cultural comparison. Many of the texts are from the Internet, others come from publications such as the *Economist* and *Fortune* magazine. The listening passages in this section are generally used to give examples for students to discuss and then practise; unit 3, *Organization*, for example, includes a comparison of American and Saudi management culture, which students analyse before describing their own country's (or company's) management culture.

Meetings

Unit 2 is entirely on the theme of meetings and practises the language and expressions students will need. The *Meetings* section in each unit is designed to give students practice in the dynamics of a meeting, and is contextualized around the unit theme. In business life meetings are quite likely to be informal and unprepared; the *Meetings* section allows for this and the approach can be varied. The scenarios may be used either for a formal meeting, which students can prepare for by setting an agenda, and follow up with minutes, or more simply as an extended discussion. In the majority of cases, students are not asked to be anyone but themselves and very little time needs to be allocated to reading background information and preparing roles.

On page 159 of the Student's Book there is a series of useful meetings phrases. Not all these phrases are likely to be used in everyday meetings, but are useful for students to fall back on if in difficulty. If you can, try to attend meetings with your students to see the kinds of problems they encounter.

Table Talk

It may seem odd for a book on business English to cover subjects as diverse as politics, genetic engineering, football, and the family. These are, however, just the kind of subjects that business people do talk about over the lunch or dinner table. It is in social situations such as at the restaurant when students often experience most difficulty in expressing themselves in English. In a strictly working environment they can control the conversation more easily and they may already know the technical vocabulary required. But outside the work situation the conversation can move in any direction.

This section is based on a listening passage; the majority of these are unscripted improvisations which include all the hesitations, interruptions, and deviations of natural speech, and as such are more demanding than the listening exercises elsewhere in the unit.

Appendices

Information gap activities

These provide the material for pair and group tasks, answer keys to quizzes, and other information referred to within the units. The section is divided into *Student A*, *Student B* (and one *Student C*), and *Extra information* for all students.

Reference section

This consists largely, but not entirely, of grammar notes on the points covered in the *Language work* sections. Also included are useful expressions for different situations, and sections on areas of difficulty such as numbers and easily confused words.

Tapescripts

These appear in the Student's Book for ease of use during lessons and later reference. The tapescripts are numbered continuously, on the cassette symbol 1.4 in the Student's and Teacher's Books, and on the cassette itself.

TEACHER'S BOOK

This Teacher's Book follows the order of the Student's Book and uses the same section headings. In addition, the first section of the teaching notes, *Warm-up*, consists of two alternative short activities to start the lesson off. These could be omitted if the *Did you know?* section is itself being used as a warm-up activity.

Comprehensive teaching notes are provided for all exercises, along with background business notes where appropriate. Answers to exercises in the Student's Book are provided in a tinted box for ease of reference; these are placed along with the teaching notes for the exercise they accompany. Occasionally suggestions are given for charts, tables, etc. to be written on the board. The reading passages in the Student's Book do not, on the whole, include comprehension questions; these are provided in the Teacher's Book for the more challenging passages, in case students are finding the material difficult.

Photocopiable activities

There are photocopiable activities for the *Warm-up* in units 5 and 8; these are on pages 74 and 75.

Progress tests

The Teacher's Book includes five photocopiable tests, each covering three units (test 5 covers units 13–14). Each test carries 100 marks and should last around 45–50 minutes, making it suitable to use during a lesson. Answers to the tests follow test 5.

CASSETTES

Two cassettes accompany the Student's Book. They provide listening comprehension tasks, speech production activites (which come at the beginning of the *Language work* section of each unit), and improvisations in the *Table talk* section.

1 PROTOCOL

The aim of this unit is for students to get to know each other, and for you to get to know them and something about their needs. There are a variety of warm-up activities for you to choose from. You might like to combine some elements from all of them. These warm-ups are longer than other warm-up activities in the rest of the book, and you may prefer to consider doing one or more of them as an optional first lesson.

First of all, however, begin by introducing yourself, but only with your name – don't add any further details. Ask students to write down three questions which they would consider suitable for asking someone at first meeting. Choose students at random, who then select one of their questions to ask you. Most students will have written fairly similar questions. You can ask them to add other questions and you can add whatever details about yourself that fit their questions.

WARM-UP

1 Names, countries, and jobs (for open groups, students who have not previously met, mono- or multilingual students)

Arrange desks into one big table. Students sit around this table and one by one introduce themselves, saying their name, country (or town), and job. They have 15 seconds to do this.

Now ask students to turn their chairs around so that they are all facing outwards from the table. They have 3 minutes to write down as many details as they can about the other students.

They turn back to the table and find out the details they couldn't remember, speaking directly to other students and using phrases such as:

I'm sorry I didn't catch your first name.

Did you say you were from Germany?

So, you're a financial director, are you?

2 Appearances (for multilingual groups)

Students should look at people sitting around their table and try and guess what nationality they are and what their interests might be. They then introduce themselves, giving their name, town, country and job. They then ask each other questions to confirm, or not, their hypotheses about each other's interests. Students should bear in mind how we make judgements on the basis of appearance and national stereotypes.

2 Culture shock (for in-company students, most of whom already know each other)

First of all, check that everyone knows each other. If not, ask students to introduce two people to each other

Put students in groups and ask them to imagine they are officials from a government department. They have been sent to a remote island in the Pacific where a small group of people, descendants from their country, have been found. Their ancestors were shipwrecked there in 1507 and their clothes, homes, language and customs have hardly changed since then. As a number of the islanders have a rare disease, they are being shipped back to their country of origin for treatment. Students have to prepare them for life in the twenty-first century when they return. Ask students to make a list of about twenty cultural traits in their country and arrange them in two columns: traits they may still share; new traits (things unknown in 1507).

The idea of this exercise is to get students to discover and analyse their own national identity and to discuss how different or 'strange' their national characteristics and norms may appear to outsiders.

DID YOU KNOW?

Before students read this section, ask them what the word protocol means to them and how important they think business etiquette is. Ask them if they can give examples of business etiquette in their own country. The photo shows a traditional Maori greeting.

Ask students to read the facts and to indicate the two which interested or surprised them most, and also the ones they think are the most important to know. Ask individual students to tell the rest of the class about business trips they make abroad and cultural differences they have noticed.

LANGUAGE WORK

Intonation

The focus here is on expressing interest, and highlighting key words to show where the interest lies: in the other person, their work activity, confirmation of what they've said, etc.

1 Students read through the written dialogues first then work with a partner as instructed. You could choose a pair of students to read one of the dialogues, then ask the rest of the class to comment on the way they said it.

2 ⌷1.1⌷ Play the tape. Students can practise saying the dialogues again or you may prefer to have your class repeat parts of the dialogues after the tape, in chorus or individually.

3 ⌷1.2⌷ Play the tape for students to do the exercise as instructed.

1 I	5 I	9 B
2 I	6 B	10 B
3 B	7 I	11 I
4 I	8 B	12 B

You could play the tape again and ask students to say the same statements expressing the opposite reaction to the speakers on the tape.

4 Ask students to give examples of words and gesture used in their country to express interest or boredom. If your class is multinational, ask the other students to guess what emotion is being expressed.

Employment history

Present perfect vs past simple

1 Students work alone and read the CV and sentences. They can discuss the answers to questions 1–3 in pairs. Correct together.

1 The past simple must be used in sentences **a** and **b** as both of these actions are past, finished and dated.
2 In sentences **c** and **d**, *have* and *work* indicate connection to the present; leave and start show that these activities are past, completed and have no connection to the present.
3 The present perfect is used in **e** because we know that she is still working for Meta 4. In sentence **f**, the present perfect is used with the phrase *this is the first time*. Remind students that the present perfect is used after *this is the first, second, third, only … time I've done something*.

2 Students should complete the exercise alone. Correct together for tenses before doing the interview. First, brainstorm students on why we ask questions: to begin a conversation, to break the ice, to show interest in someone.

Students should be familiar with the tenses reviewed in this exercise. If there are still any problems in this area, go through page 165 in the Reference section at the back of the book.

1 What school … did you attend? Why did you choose …?
2 How many jobs have you had since you left school?
3 What did you do …?
4 How long have you been …?
5 Have you been …?
6 … which have you found …? (*do you find* is also correct.)
7 … you have ever made …?
8 When was the last meeting that you attended? Did you use …?
9 Have you ever had to do …?
10 … you have done?

Greetings

1 【1.3】 Play the tape for students to do the exercise as instructed. Students write answers alone then discuss them in pairs. If answers vary, ask students to explain their opinions.

> 1   India
> 2   Japan
> 3   Canada / USA

2 If your class is multinational, put students from different cultures together in pairs to discuss these questions. At the end, compare differences with other pairs or the class as a whole.

3 Students work alone. Correct together.

> 2   B, I 6   E, I 10 E, F
> 3   B, F 7   B, I 11 E, I
> 4   E, F 8   E, I 12 E,
> 5   E, I 9   E, F

You could extend the exercise to include the sentence probably used immediately before or after these phrases. For example, Well, *thanks again. Oh, not at all. Call me back if you need more information …*

Telephone etiquette

1 Students complete the exercise as instructed

> Suggested alternative expressions
> (there are others):
>
> 1   *Hello. May I help you?*
> 2   *May I speak to Mr Lee, please?*
> 3   *Who's speaking, please?*
> 4   *Richard Gabbertas from Meta 4 speaking.*
> 5   *Sorry, could you repeat your name, please?*
> 6   *And what's the name of your company, please?*
> 7   *I'll try and connect you.*
> 8   *Sorry, the line's busy.*
> 9   *Could you hold the line, please?*
> 10 *No, could I leave a message please?*

> 11 *Yes, certainly.*
> 12 *Can I have your number, please?*
> 13 *OK, I'll pass on your message.*
> 14 *any thanks for your help. Goodbye.*

2 【1.4】 Students listen to the tape. First, with books closed, they should concentrate on differences in information given. Then, with books open, they should listen for differences in the expressions used. They should compare them with the alternative expressions they wrote in the previous exercise.

3 If you have a phone in your classroom and access to another room with a phone, use real phones to role-play this conversation. If not, ask students to sit back to back for the role-play.

BUSINESS SKILLS

Social culture

Students should read and discuss all the points in the passage. Point 1 could be extended to the difference between Holland and the Netherlands, America and the USA, etc. Find out from your class who has visited the UK and what parts of the passage they can relate to. Did they visit pubs? Did they make any mistakes like joking about royalty, or getting too personal? Were they struck by anything *not* mentioned in the passage? You may wish to point out the American spelling of *offense* and *favorite*.

1 Students can use dictionaries to check any of the words and phrases in italics that they don't know.

slang:	very informal language
grumble:	complain
off limits:	not considered acceptable
blow your own trumpet:	boast
bear hugs:	displays of friendship by throwing your arms around someone and squeezing tightly
ice-breaking:	reducing tension at a first meeting

② If your class is multinational, put students from different countries together for this exercise. Give them some time alone first to prepare questions.

Business culture

① Students complete the exercise as instructed.

② [1.5] Play the tape for students to do the matching exercise.

1 3	3 a	5 f
2 b	4 c	6 d

③ Discussion in pairs or class as a whole. Students may like certain aspects of the business woman's working situation as opposed to their own. Which parts would they swap and why? Ask students if they can think of other aspects of working life which differ from hers. For example, do colleagues socialize with each other outside work in their countries? Is it common to invite the boss for dinner to their homes?

Small talk

① Brainstorm students on the meaning of *small talk* and why it is useful. Ask students if they find small talk difficult and what tricks they use to keep the conversation going. Elicit from students: small talk is the three or four minutes you spend chatting with a person before getting down to business. It has several uses, such as:

– giving you time to get used to someone's voice if it's your first meeting
– giving you both time to calm down and relax
– establishing contact (*breaking the ice*) with a new person or re-establishing contact with a previous acquaintance
– finding out personal information about the person, which may then help you to do business with them.

1 [1.6] Before playing the tape, ask students what objects in a person's office can be used to help start a conversation, and what questions can be asked.

Play the tape and elicit how the visitor managed to incorporate the details of the office into the conversation.

Ask students to suggest other objects. Write the names of these down on a card and divide the class into hosts and visitors. Students take turns to ask questions inspired by their partner's 'objects'.

2 Students discuss the question in pairs. Ask what subjects are topical at the moment in students' countries. Is there a major sporting event, or strange weather for the season, or a political crisis or scandal?

3–4 Students do the role-play as instructed. Ask pairs of students to volunteer to act out their role-play in front of the rest of the class.

You could ask your class to stand up and mingle, trying to spend a minimum of four minutes making small talk with different students. Ask them if they found it easier to talk to certain students than to others. Did they have problems finding a subject in common with some students? Could they have gone on talking for longer with others?

② To help students, you could give your class an example of how you would answer this question by writing up the figure on the board and completing it for yourself. You can extend the exercise from work life to personal life for students who already know each other well.

1 As instructed.

2 Students could ask questions such as:

How have the early events in your life affected your present life?

How do the past events differ from your predicted future events?

Test your protocol

One of the ideas behind this exercise is to show how little most of us know about other cultures. Students may dispute some of the answers since the answers themselves are very general and obviously don't apply to every inhabitant of the countries in question.

You may like to give students practice of nationalities and languages by quickly going through the countries in the quiz, e.g. Egypt, Egyptian, Arabic. You could also review the use of the definite article with some countries and languages.

Students can do the quiz alone or with a partner. They should then compare their answers before checking with the key on page 147 of the Student's Book. Finally, discuss the remaining questions.

MEETINGS

See the Introduction on page 6 for ideas on running classroom meetings.

Students should read the abridged article alone, then comment on the joint venture. Do they know of other similar cases in their country or elsewhere?

Following the instructions in the Student's Book, decide if you are going to follow step 1 or 2. If you have a large class, put your students into groups of four. Students may want a few minutes alone to think about the advantages of the company they have chosen as a suitable business partner. In step 1, one student from each group could be elected chairperson.

Whether you opt for step 1 or 2, you could follow up by having a discussion on the practicalities of the two companies joining forces, e.g. how the information would be be made public, or advertised. One member of each group could announce the joint venture, using the quote by Colin Whaley in the article.

As a writing activity, you could ask you class to write a summary of the decisions made during this discussion.

TABLE TALK

① See the Introduction on page 6 for the rationale behind this section. Students should read the table alone first. Ask students which statistics interested them most.

Let students discuss the questions in groups, or if you prefer, as a whole class. Take advantage of this discussion to introduce or review debating and arguing language. So as not to interrupt the discussion, make a note of expressions students could have used, and go over them after the discussion. Students will have plenty of opportunity to use them again in later units.

Don't forget to make a note of good English expressions you hear so that you can share them with students who didn't know them before.

Make a note of important mistakes or intonation problems and correct quickly afterwards.

② Ask groups for their ideas and write them up on the board. If they need help, here are some typical ones (including ones which may be taboo in some cultures):

– the arts	– money
– cars	– politics
– children	– race
– criticism of society	– religion
– dialects	– royal family
– drugs	– sex
– education	– shopping
– family	– social conditions
– fashion	– sport
– food and drink	– taxes
– gardening	– television
– health	– the economy
– house prices	– travel
– information technology	– weather
	– women

1.7 Listen to the tape as instructed. Play the tape completely the first time while students take notes. Play it a second time and ask students to say Stop! each time a subject is mentioned. Then discuss if the speaker said the subject was suitable or not, and if it would be suitable or not in students' countries.

2 MEETINGS

This unit takes students through the different stages of holding / attending meetings: why we have meetings; what makes a meeting effective or not; the language needed depending on whether the meeting is formal or informal; and finishes with hands-on practice in carrying out a meeting in English.

WARM-UP

 Effective meetings

Ask students to work out approximately how many hours they spend in meetings. Then ask them to brainstorm what makes a meeting either effective or ineffective and to list these points in order of importance. Meetings are often criticized as being a waste of time or unproductive; however, for many students they are a regular and necessary part of their jobs. Elicit the positive and negative aspects of meetings generally. Find out how meetings are conducted in your students' departments and how effective they feel they are. Ask if their meetings are formal / informal, if someone takes minutes, if votes are cast, etc.

② Alternatives to meetings

Ask students to discuss alternatives to meetings. However, there is one major constraint on their discussion: they mustn't use the pronoun *I*. Let students talk in pairs for two minutes before brainstorming:

- how many of them were able to avoid using *I*
- why we find it so difficult not to use *I*
- how students feel about listening to someone who starts every sentence with *I* (or equivalent in their own language)
- if they didn't use *I*, how they managed to avoid it.

DID YOU KNOW?

Students read through all the facts and quotes alone. Some of these (particularly 3 and 10) will confirm or not what was discussed during the warm-up. Ask students to give their opinions on the quotes and find out if the statistics apply to their jobs or departments.

Next, find out who has and has not attended meetings (both with or without native English participants). Put students into balanced groups of those with experience and those without. The latter should ask the former about their most successful, most disastrous, and most or least useful meeting.

LANGUAGE WORK

Stress

1 Students do the exercise as instructed.

2 [2.1] Play the tape, stopping after each sentence if necessary, to let students check their answers.

1 destination / vehicle	3 Susy / ever
2 Before / now	4 you / Pete

You could ask students to underline different words, including words not in italics, to see how this changes the meaning of the sentences.

② [2.2] Students do the exercise as instructed.

1 a	3 c
2 c	4 a

③ Students work in pairs and take turns to read the sentences in exercise 2 with one of the remaining meanings. Check that they are placing the stress on the right word in the sentences and correct if necessary.

④ If available, use real phones from the classroom to a nearby room, if not students can sit back to back. Students can review the telephone language in Unit 1 if necessary.

Hypothesizing
Second and third conditional

Ask your class to read and study sentences **a** to **f** alone.

1 This exercise sets the model for the majority of grammar exercises in this book. See the Introduction, page 5, for the rationale behind such exercises. Students analyse the sentences. Correct together. If your class has problems with the conditional, go through page 155 in the Reference section with them.

> **a** and **c** refer to the present and future
> **e** and **f** refer to the present and the past
> **b** and **d** refer to the past

2 Students complete the sentences alone then compare with a neighbour. Check that everyone has used the correct conditional form.

> Possible answers:
> 1 If everyone was paid the same salary, no one would work late!
> 2 If I hadn't joined this company, I would have set up a business myself.
> 3 The company might have had higher profits last year if we hadn't launched that unsuccessful model.
> 4 If I were the boss, I would move the premises into town.
> 5 The employees would work with more satisfaction if they received more praise.
> 6 If I had founded this company, I wouldn't be in this job now!

3 Ask students to read through the three ideas to keep meetings effective and to discuss the question. Also ask them which idea they prefer; if they have any experience of any of the ideas; and if they can think of any other novel ways of holding meetings. Which idea does the photo in the Student's Book refer to?

2.3 Play the tape once. Ask students to tell you the words the speakers used that helped them find the answers.

> 1 extract 3
> 2 extract 2
> 3 extract 1

Business etiquette

Students complete the quiz alone. You may like to organize a class survey and ask one student to write up all the answers on the board in the form of a table, then discuss the results.

If your students all know each other well, you could let them add personalized answers to the questions. Ask them to write the answers on a separate piece of paper, then gather up the anonymous quizzes and ask them to guess who wrote which answers!

Once students have finished the quiz, elicit suitable expressions for relevant situations, e.g.:

I'm sorry I'm late, but I got held up in traffic. (1b)
This is on me. (8a)

If your class is multinational, you could discuss how different cultures act in the situations presented in the quiz.

BUSINESS SKILLS
Being prepared

1 Students read the text alone.

1 In pairs, they discuss, or look up in dictionaries, the meaning of the words in italics. They could find synonyms in English for these words, or translate them into their own language.

attendees:	people attending a meeting
scheduled:	arranged for a certain time
senior:	higher in rank
descending order of rank:	beginning with the most senior person
counterparts:	person with the same level of seniority in another company
dress code:	standard of dress required

formal business attire:	suits and ties (in an international context)	
refreshments:	food and drink	
jump into the business at hand:	start the business of the meeting straight away, without introduction	
see them off:	say goodbye	

2 If your class is multinational, put students from different countries together to do this activity. You could ask someone whose culture is quite different from the rest of the class to give a short presentation about preparing meetings in their country.

2 [2.4] Let students read questions 1 and 2 before playing the tape.

1 Write two columns on the board: *Chinese* and *Australian*. After playing the tape, ask one student to elicit from others the differences they heard, and to write them in the columns.

	Chinese	Australian
preparation	thorough	minimal
	agenda agreed and circulated beforehand	agenda not necessary
	only those invited will attend	people often attend without forewarning
	refreshments provided	
formality	punctuality important; attendees expected to be early and meetings end on time	little formality or ritual; punctuality respected but not vital
	introductions performed according to hierarchy	flexibility important; seniority not apparent from appearance or behaviour

	dress is always formal	dress is usually formal
small talk	important in order to break the ice	enjoyed up to a point, particularly about sport and politics, but being direct is valued

2 Meetings are seen as an opportunity for discussion and are flexible in terms of time and the subjects discussed.

Controlling a meeting

① The best overall tactic is to have a chairperson who sends out a memo in advance with the meeting agenda (with items in order of priority) clearly stating that the meeting must / will start and end at the specified time. Native speakers should be made aware of the level of English of the participants and should be careful not to direct discussion only to those who speak English well. The chairperson should also defuse conflicts by bringing in other opinions, alert participants who are straying from the subject, and summarize from time to time particularly at the end. Long meetings should be punctuated with breaks.

② Students discuss ways of implementing an evaluation system as instructed. If they need help, you could suggest that if companies had a system in which people spent the last five minutes of the meeting discussing how it had gone, the results might be:

– many meetings could be avoided as unneccessary
– attendees would be better prepared
– overall time spent in meetings would be reduced.

Getting down to business

Students work alone. Correct together.

You may wish to discuss with your students which of the expressions are mainly suitable for use in formal business meetings (2, 4, 5, 6). You could also ask them to suggest alternative expressions.

> a 1, 3, 8
> b 4, 5, 6
> c 2, 7

Agreeing, supporting, countering

Students read the expressions and underline or highlight the ones they use. Although it is important for students to understand all of these expressions, everyone has their own personality and way of speaking, so it is always good advice to students to encourage them to use words and expressions they feel comfortable using in English, or which correspond most to the way they speak in their own language. If you understand your students' own language, ask them to tell you the expressions they usually use in their language and find the English equivalent for them.

1 First, discuss all the problems in the cartoon in the Student's Book. Ask why the meeting is likely to have been a waste of time. Then students read through the options in the table and choose the best and worst scenarios.

2 Ask students to compare in groups, or class as a whole.

Interrupting, recapping, confirming, moving on

As with the previous section, students read through the expressions, choosing the phrases they prefer, or adding others.

Students then read the points in the flow chart in their book and, working in groups of three or four, express their opinions using the expressions from the table.

The flow chart allows groups of different numbers to work through the activity. If there are four students, Student A gives his / her opinion of point

1 (organization of lessons). Student B interrupts, Student C summarizes, Student D confirms, and Student A then carries on with point 2 (time spent speaking and listening).

With fewer students, Student A will speak again earlier in the process, e.g. if there are three students Student A will confirm and Student B will start with point 2. If there are two students they will take turns throughout.

Concluding

1 [2.5] Play the tape. Students should base their answers on the intonation of the speakers as well as what they say.

> Meeting 3 ends on a less positive note than 1 and 2.

2 Ask your class to read questions 1–5 before playing the tape. You may need to play the tape twice, or stop after the expressions used to conclude a meeting, to give them time to write them down.

> 1 Formal: I think we can draw this meeting to a close.
>   Informal: I think we can call it a day then.
> 2 Does anybody have anything to add?
>   Is everyone else clear about what we've agreed to do?
> 3 meeting 2
> 4 meeting 3
> 5 so that everyone goes away with a clear idea of what has been decided and consequently what has to be done

MEETINGS

First of all, give students time to read through the situation and the proposed solutions. They should analyse the factors involved in each situation. For example, from an employer's point of view, job sharing could increase insurance contributions and pensions, and involve extra training; sabbaticals involve organizing someone to take over, paying two salaries, and employing extra staff on a temporary basis; a four-day week can complicate work timetables, etc. (If students have difficulty thinking of ideas, do exercise 8 in Unit 2 of the Workbook as a preparatory exercise.)

Organize your class into groups of four if possible. If not, you can double up roles, i.e. have two workers, or two trade union members, for larger classes. For smaller classes, you can eliminate one of the workers.

The member of new management should open the meeting and present the solutions to the others. This person should also control and conclude the meeting.

Encourage students to use the expressions studied in the previous sections of this unit. Make a note of important or frequent mistakes and correct once the activity is finished.

Find out which decision each group came to and ask them to analyse how well they conducted their meeting.

As a writing activity, you could ask students to write up the minutes of their meeting.

TABLE TALK

1 [2.6] Before playing the tape, warn students that they may find the American (who speaks more) easier to understand, and therefore they may be able to complete more of the *USA* column than the *UK* column. Answers are based on what the speakers say!

	USA	UK
1	four years	five years
2	fixed	flexible
3	fixed to two terms	flexible, no limit
4	no pressure in second term	—

	USA	UK
5	Two: Republican, Democratic	Three main parties: Conservative, Labour, Liberal Democrats, plus other small parties
6	Democrats	Labour
7	Republican	Conservative
8	Republicans: national outlook Democrats: world outlook	—

2 If your class is multinational, students from different countries should do this exercise together.

Students can also discuss:

– the advantages and disadvantages of proportional representation vs the 'first past the post' system in the UK
– to what extent the way politicians conduct their private life is indicative of their public capacity
– the media's relationship with politicians in different countries.

1 Students read the sectors then fill in the pie chart according to how they think money should be allocated to these sectors in their country.

2 Students discuss their budget in groups.

You could also ask your students to work in pairs or groups and do the same activity for other countries, for example developing African nations, or overpopulated countries, etc.

3 ORGANIZATION

WARM-UP

1 Describing the organization

Find out how much students know about their company organization – how many employees, managers, departments, etc. are there? Ask students to draw a simple geometrical diagram of the way their company or department is organized. Students can then compare their interpretations. With in-company courses, you could ask one student to draw the diagram on the board, guided by the other members of the class. Ask if this structure has been the same for a long time or if it has changed recently. Are there big changes to organization when a new CEO or Managing Director takes over?

2 Reforming the organization

Ask students to discuss briefly what would be the one change that they would like to see implemented in their organization or company, which would most enhance their working life. They may suggest changes to their environment rather than factors such as money or promotion. Discuss the implications of students' choices.

DID YOU KNOW?

Before reading the facts, focus students' attention on the symbols in the illustration.

The triangle is the simplest form of showing company structure; it represents a hierarchical structure with the power centred on a small number of people at the top of the triangle. A more elaborate version of this is the series of small triangles inside a larger one, which shows smaller hierarchies of similar size, each with its internal structure, within the main system.

The series of circles shows a more fluid system, with groups of different sizes represented by the small circles operating freely inside the larger circle which represents the company as a whole. This could also show a number of subsidiaries within a parent company.

The matrix represents the most fluid structure, with the emphasis on the task rather than the hierarchy. The dots show individuals or groups who can function at different levels according to the requirements of the task.

The spider's web shows the most intricate structure, with power emanating out from the centre and links between all levels.

Ask them which one comes closest to the way they see their company. They can then discuss the advantages and disadvantages of each structure system, decide which system would suit them best, and whether organizations of the future are likely to get bigger or smaller.

Ask students to cover the page and guess the answers to the following questions:

- How many hours does the average person spend working a year?
- When were open plan offices introduced?
- Which food company is the most foreign-orientated in the world?
- Which countries have the longest holidays?
- By 2010 what percentage of the workforce will be over the age of 45?

Students uncover the facts to find the answers and read the other information. Discuss together.

As an extra activity, you could tell students to close their books and ask them what some of the different numbers, dates and percentages refer to.

LANGUAGE WORK

Vowel sounds

1 3.1 Play the tape for students to listen to the pairs of words as instructed. If students have difficulty with the vowel sounds, say them yourself first. Ask students to watch the movement of your mouth as you say them and to imitate you.

2 Students do the activity as instructed.

/ɜː/	/ɔː/	/eə/	/eɪ/
work	walk	their	they
first	forced	shared	shade

2 Students work alone or in pairs to do questions 1 and 2, but will probably have to speak out loud to find the stress and the vowel sounds!

3 **3.2** Play the tape for students to check their answers, and correct together afterwards.

1	2
<u>cir</u>cuit: /ɜː/	<u>back</u>date: /eɪ/
dis<u>turb</u>: /ɜː/	<u>chair</u>man: /eə/
<u>for</u>mat: /ɔː/	com<u>pare</u>: /eə/
<u>law</u>yer: /ɔː/	de<u>lay</u>: /eɪ/
<u>pur</u>pose: /ɜː/	ex<u>change</u>: /eɪ/
se<u>cure</u>: /ɔː/ (but	<u>fail</u>ure: /eɪ/
/ʊə/ is also	<u>state</u>ment: /eɪ/
possible)	<u>ware</u>house: /eə/
sup<u>port</u>: /ɔː/	

Company history

Present perfect simple vs present perfect continuous

Students read the pairs of sentences alone. Explain that the words in italics are clues to the answers.

1 Elicit rules from students for when you should and shouldn't use the present perfect continuous. This is still a tricky area for many students at this level; their own language will determine how difficult they find this. The general underlying principle is that the present perfect continuous looks at *activities*, while the simple form looks at the *result*.

You should use the present perfect continuous:
– when you want to emphasize that the action / situation is of long duration and unfinished, e.g. **d**
– when the activity / situation is temporary, e.g. **f**
– when the action is in progress and is not complete, e.g. **l**

You shouldn't use the present perfect continuous:
– when the activity / situation has just finished or is complete, e.g. **a**
– when you want to talk about a more permanent situation, e.g. **c**.

As an extension, you could ask students to suggest ways of continuing the sentences, e.g. *I've had this office for six months now, and it still hasn't been redecorated.*

Go through the explanation on page 165 in the Reference section.

2 Students work alone to do the exercise as instructed. Correct together.

1 has grown
2 have seen
3 has opened
4 has increased
5 has also been pushing
   (the process has not finished)
6 have been pulling (the action is
   temporary, and may not be complete)

Answer any questions concerning vocabulary in this text, then discuss the question below the article.

ensuing:	following
globalize:	penetrate markets throughout world
diversify:	vary the product range
subsidiaries:	smaller companies controlled by a parent company
facilities:	factories
peripherals:	extra equipment used with a computer but not part of it

Jobs, work, and responsibilities

① Students do the exercise as instructed.

1 job	4 jobs
2 work	5 work
3 Work	

You could ask students to think of some verb and adjective collocations for these two words, e.g.:

a badly-paid job	*to find work*
a demanding job	*to set to work*
a stable job	*to look for work*
to get a job	*to go to work*
to apply for a job	

Discuss the questions and quotations in the exercise with students. Ask them to talk about the worst job they've ever had.

② Students can work in pairs or small groups to do this exercise. Go through the grammar of superlatives if necessary.

Company profile

① Students complete the quiz alone, then discuss their answers with a partner, in groups, or class as a whole. Students could invent other questions, or you could extend the quiz by writing the following questions on the board:

---

1 Would this company be:
  a your own with no partners
  b yours with partners
  c privately owned by someone else
  d state-owned?
2 Would it be:
  a local
  b national
  c international?
3 How would you organize working hours?
4 Would it be run by men or women?
5 What field of business would you choose?

---

② Students work alone to do the matching exercise. Correct together. Note that students will hear the words in the following exercise.

1 b	3 d	5 c
2 a	4 e	6 f

③ [3.3]

1 Play the tape once so students can listen to the answers and then decide what the questions might have been.

2 Students look at the questions and see how many they guessed correctly. Play the tape once more so that they can match the answers with the questions.

a 3	c 5	e 1
b 6	d 2	f 4

As a writing activity, students could summarize what the financial director said.

3 Students do the activity as instructed. Encourage students to use each other's answers to extend the 'interview'. You could then ask each pair to present their partner's company history.

BUSINESS SKILLS

Describing your company

① Students work in pairs to do the exercise as instructed. If they have difficulty, write the headings below on the board and turn the activity into a matching exercise.

Company history:	2, 10
Size:	5, 7, 11
Current activities:	3, 9
Location:	4, 6, 8
Key area of business:	1, 12

② Give students enough time to prepare the draft of their speech. Encourage them to use expressions such as:

First I'd like to talk about …

Now I'd like to move on to …

Finally …

Students should compare their drafts, to correct or improve them.

Ask individual students to volunteer to make their speeches in front of the rest of the class.

Management

3.4 Give students time to read the questions before playing the tape. Play the tape once, then a second time, stopping between questions if necessary, to give students time to write notes for the answers. Correct together. If students disagree about answers, look at the tapescript at the back of the Student's Book or play parts of the tape again to confirm answers.

Saudi	US
1 great	small
2 very	not very
3 yes	yes
4 not very important	obsessive
5 at a leisurely pace	as quickly as possible
6 people	task

Finish off with the writing activity as instructed.

Strategy and analysis

1 Students do the matching exercise alone.

a 6	c 4	e 3
b 5	d 1	f 2

2 – 3 Choose one or other of these questions depending on your group. Students can work in pairs or groups. Encourage them to work on each point fully before going on to the following one. Ask individual students to volunteer to present their definitions to the rest of the class. For exercise 2, encourage students to agree or disagree with each other.

MEETINGS

Let students read the two quotations, and comment on them. Make sure everyone has understood the texts and the aim of the meeting.

The texts contradict each other; which, if either, reflects their own experience of teamwork?

If you have a large class, organize students into smaller groups. Remind them to use the meetings expressions learned in Unit 2 and on page 159 of the Student's Book.

Ask one person in each group to 'hold' the meeting and control the discussion, making sure that each member of the group has a chance to give their opinion.

For Exercise 3, use students' current projects if they are all from the same company. If they are from different companies, they may prefer to discuss past projects.

Another member of each group could take notes which could be photocopied at the end of the meeting, given to each member within the group, then used to write a report or minutes of the meeting.

TABLE TALK

1 3.5 You may prefer to do this exercise in three parts, playing each section of the tape twice before going on to the next section. You should point out to students that *school*, *college*, and *university* mean different things in the UK and USA. Americans use the word *school* to refer to what the British call *college*, and an American *college* is a British *university*.

USA	UK	Japan
1 18 / 19	18	18 / 19
2 yes: SAT	yes: A-levels	yes: very difficult exams

USA	UK	Japan
3 student	government and student / family	student / family
4 4 / 5 years	3 / 4 years	4 years
5 3 to 1	high in years 1–2; in year 3 students don't have time to socialize	50 / 50

For more detailed answers, use the tapescript on page 174 of the Student's Book.

Students then complete the table for their own country.

2 Students do the exercise as instructed. If students are of different nationalities, they could prepare a formal five-minute presentation outlining the education system in their country. As education is often a lively subject of debate in many countries, you could ask students how they feel about the standard of schools and universities in their country. If they have children, are they satisfied with the education they are receiving? Is there a public and private education system? How do they differ? Explain that *public* schools in the USA are publicly financed, i.e. non-fee-paying, while in Britain they are private, fee-paying, and often residential (*boarding* schools).

4 NUMBERS

WARM-UP

① Number recognition

Find out from students who uses numbers in English at work and what sort of numbers they say and hear.

Discuss the various problems of saying and understanding numbers. Do they find it difficult to understand numbers when taking information on the phone, or when they hear numbers out of context? Do students always know what the number refers to? It could be a phone number, a sum of money, an order, or even the weather. Brainstorm different types of numbers and check number recognition. You could write these examples on the board:

0832 2564 2541 3254	a credit card number
BA5489	a flight number
BE12 6KH	a British postal code
CA 58974	a US zip code
30°C or 85°F	temperatures

Ask students what sort of numbers they see on an invoice, on a letter, a plane ticket, etc. For an invoice, elicit *account number*, *invoice number*, *quantity*, *amount*, *discount*.

② Decimal vs duodecimal

Ask students if they know the origin of the decimal system and what they consider to be the advantages and disadvantages of both systems. Do they feel that the UK, USA, and the few remaining countries still using the duodecimal system should adopt the metric system throughout? Does it create problems at work for your class? Discuss other differences between the USA / UK and the rest of the world, such as commas and stops in fractions, and days and months in dates.

DID YOU KNOW?

Ask students to read through the facts silently. Check new vocabulary. Read facts 2–4 to confirm or complete warm-up exercise 2. Ask which facts they already knew or which ones surprised them most.

If your class is multilingual, you could focus on fact 8. Find out what numbers are considered lucky or unlucky in the countries represented in the group. The numbers 4 and 9 are unlucky in Japan as these words also mean *death* and *pain* respectively.

You could also ask students to discuss fact 10 and find other examples of products named with numbers, e.g. Levi 501 jeans, Peugeot 106, Boeing 747.

LANGUAGE WORK

Saying numbers

① Although it may seem inappropriate at this level to be practising the difference between *thirteen* and *thirty*, you may be surprised at how many students still have difficulty in this area.

You could do the following exercise to practise this. Write on the board in two columns:

1	2
13	30
14	40
15	50
16	60
17	70
18	80
19	90

Say numbers from the columns at random and ask students to say whether the number is from column 1 or 2. Ask individual students to call out numbers.

You could then dictate some dates and ask students to read them back, e.g. *1530, 1990, 1618, 1750.*

4.1 Students read sentences 1–7. Play the tape once. Students could compare their answers with a partner. If answers are very different, play the tape again. Correct together. Ask individual students to say the sentences.

1	30	5		bin
2	30	6		computer's chip
3	16	7		heat
4	17			

2 Students do the exercise as instructed.

You could, at this point, also do a number dictation if you feel your class could use this extra practice. Tell students you're going to say each number twice. Students read back the numbers afterwards for correction. Suggested dictation:

12,890	*6,015*	*78,005*
31st	*13th*	*30th*
12th	*26.9*	*0.5678*
⁷⁄₈	*²⁄₃*	*12½*
11.50 am	*3.30 pm*	*8.45 pm*

Articles and nouns
The definite article

Ask students to read the example sentences alone.

1 Students can volunteer explanations about the use of the definite article in the sentences. The rules are given on page 156 in the Reference section.

2 Before beginning this exercise, revise the difference between countable and uncountable nouns. Students may have learnt this using the terms *mass* and *count*, or simply *singular* and *plural*. The important thing is that they understand that one can be seen as being clearly separated into parts and the other can't. Give obvious examples such as *water* as opposed to *glasses of water*, then less obvious examples such as *money* as opposed to *coins*, and also *time vs minutes*.

Students mark the words alone, as instructed, then compare with a partner. Correct together.

C:	2, 7, 8, b, c, d, e, g
U:	1, 3, 4, 5, 6, a
C / U:	f, h (C: a scientific paper, a work of art)

Students then do the matching activity. Give one example if necessary, e.g. **4** goes with **b**: we can count *bags*, but *luggage* is considered a mass. We don't say *one luggage, two luggages*, etc., but *two pieces of luggage*.

1	g	5	d
2	h	6	e
3	c	7	f
4	b	8	a

3 Students could vary answers to include adjectives or different degrees of quantity.

Suggested answers:	
some data	some knowledge of
a few pieces of luggage	a heavy piece of machinery
a piece of news	a good piece of advice
a lot of money	an overload of work

4 Students do the exercise as instructed.

1	The, —	4	—, —, the
2	some, the, —	5	a, —
3	one piece of	6	some, The

The language of trends
Prepositions

Students look at the example sentences alone.

1 Students do the exercise as instructed, using the example sentences to help them.

1	to, of	3	in
2	at	4	by

You could ask your class to make further sentences concerning their own country or company, e.g. *Our company's profits rose by 8% last year.*

2 Check that everyone understands the difference between the three words. Students can work alone or in pairs.

1 arise: come up
2 raise: bring up
3 raised: put up
4 rising: go up
raise can be replaced by *increase*
rise can be replaced by *increase* and *go up*

3 Students do the exercise as instructed and then compare with a partner. Correct together.

1 risen / gone up
2 raised / increased
3 increased
4 arisen
5 raise
6 rise

Graphs, charts, and tables

1 Focus on Figure 1. Elicit suggestions as to what the prices on the graph could represent. (The figure shows prices per barrel for crude oil.)

1 Students insert the verbs as instructed.

1 remain relatively stable
2 escalate
3 reach a peak
4 plummet
5 fluctuate
6 rise steadily

2 The discussion on the projections should involve the second conditional (Unit 2). Ask of students what effect these projections would have on their company or on them. Students can discuss in small groups, or class as a whole. If your class is multilingual, put students of different nationalities in small groups to compare effects on their countries. Ask them to discuss alternative forms of energy being used or developed in their country.

2 Focus on Figure 2, then ask students to complete the exercise. The statistics in the graph are 1995 figures.

1	a	UK	2	a	nearly
	b	Sweden		b	nothing like as high as
	c	Sweden		c	substantially
	d	Italy		d	the same as
	e	Germany		e	marginally
	f	Canada		f	approximately
	g	Sweden		g	a little less than

As a follow-up, ask students to discuss the following points:

– In Uganda nearly 50% of the population is under 15. What factors account for the difference in ages of populations? Why is the percentage of over-65s in Sweden so much higher than, for example, in Australia (11.7%)? Are the differences linked to healthy living, better medical care, eating habits, climate, working conditions?
– If your class is multilingual, ask students if they know what the figure is for their country or if they think it must be high or low, and why. Then discuss the implications of demographic change.

3 [4.2] Before playing the tape, ask students to study Figure 3. If you have not already done so, go over the rules on numbers in the Reference section, on pages 161–162, especially with regard to how numbers such as *1300* can be said. (The American speaker says *thirteen hundred*; a British speaker would probably say *one thousand three hundred*.) Also point out the use of the decimal points, as some countries use commas where we use points (see *Did you know?* section).

Play the tape once, then a second time, pausing after each number if necessary.

a	0.052	d	1300–1800	g	3.70
b	1.5	e	590	h	130
c	660	f	116	i	20p

Elicit different ways of talking about money, e.g. *one dollar ninety*. Ask students to name other currencies. Make sure everyone knows the meaning of *currency*, *change*, *exchange rate*, *money*, *coins*, *notes / bills*.

Students could comment on the statistics using *just under*, *fared much better than*, and words from the second part of exercise 2.

Ask students how the foreign exchange rate affects their companies, or them personally. Does it influence their decision to take holidays abroad? Is the currency in their country strong at the moment (be careful with this one in multinational groups)?

BUSINESS SKILLS

Presenting statistics

1 Divide students into groups of three. Allocate each student within the group one set of statistics. Instruct students to cover up the statistics of the other members of their group. Students then follow the instructions.

2 Using the original information plus what they have written themselves they should be able to make a short (2–3 minutes should be enough) presentation to the other members of their group. Monitor progress, offering help if necessary. Afterwards, students can have a general discussion, within their group, of all the statistics that have been presented.

This exercise is designed to give students practice in talking about different kinds of numbers (percentages, fractions, ratios, etc.) and also in expressing approximations. There is more detailed practice of presentations in Unit 11.

Discussing statistics

Students read the quiz questions alone, then discuss their answers or opinions with a partner. There are no correct answers; the quiz is intended to give further practice in discussing and saying numbers in a humorous context.

You could either ask students to compare answers with another pair, or alternatively organize a class survey and discuss the results. Ask one student to write up the results on the board. Discuss the points where the answers are very different.

If your class is multilingual, some answers may vary according to cultural differences or conditions in students' countries. For example, a hot summer's day will be very different for someone from a hot or cold country; a short commuter journey will be relative to the size of place your students come from.

Wrong number?

1 Discuss the quotation before students read the article. Do they agree?

1 Students work in pairs. They should use dictionaries or ask you for the meaning of the words in italics.

interim:	provisional, using information available at the time
gaffe:	mistake
malaise:	problem, feeling of unease
notorious:	well-known for some bad quality
paralyse:	cause to stop functioning
erroneous:	wrong

2 Class discussion. Elicit mistakes companies make: wrong policy, bad decisions, choosing a bad location, launching an untested product, etc.

2 **4.3** Play the tape for students to make notes as instructed.

1 taking on work you're not qualified to do
2 not finding out what government funds and facilities are available
3 putting off unpleasant decisions
4 not being flexible on prices
5 not listening to your staff
6 lack of cultural knowledge about customers

Students should rank these mistakes, then add others they have either experienced or know of.

MEETINGS

First, students should read through the proposed products 1–5. Organize students in groups of three and allocate roles. Students argue for or against the products according to their roles.

This activity could also be carried out as a class discussion. Students could choose which products they think are the most feasible, profitable, interesting, etc. and justify their arguments.

Alternatively, give small groups one product each to defend in front of the rest of the class. They should then argue against the product of the other groups.

Encourage students to talk about the consequences of these products being freely available on the market. (The items and products are real.)

TABLE TALK

4.4   Ask if anyone can tell you what they already know about the Elgin / Parthenon marbles. As instructed, students listen to the tape and answer questions 1–7. Let them read through the questions first before playing the tape. Play the tape twice, first for students to get the general sense, and again to concentrate on numbers. Students can compare answers with each other first, then correct together.

1	About 2,500 years ago
2	115
3	about 47
4	6 million
5	250
6	1816
7	Speaker B (the man)

Finish off with a discussion of questions 8 and 9.

For question 9, you could present national heritage as an argument for the return of works of art, and lack of security, exhibition space, and visitors in the country of origin as an argument against. Ask students if in their opinion works of art should go back to the country of origin even if they were bought by the country now holding them. Should all types of art be repatriated (obelisks, paintings, sculptures)? Should there be more travelling museums?

5 COMMUNICATION

WARM-UP

1 Communication test

Ask students to do the *Two-minute Test in Communication* on photocopiable page 74 of this book. Don't interrupt students while they're doing the test, even if they're not doing it correctly. Afterwards, when everyone has finished, ask for some feedback on what the test is trying to prove, i.e. that we don't read instructions carefully, and we make erroneous assumptions (if there are a lot of instructions, we assume that we have to follow them).

Now discuss some or all of the following questions:

- Why do we communicate?
- What are the main obstacles to communication?
- What are the qualities of a good communicator?

2 Success factors

Tell students that in a survey to determine factors in achieving success in business, executives were asked to place in rank order ten factors which they believed had helped them achieve their status. Dictate the ten factors below, and ask students to put them in order of importance. The idea is to discuss the importance of good communication skills (this is explored further in Unit 11).

ambition	*formal training*
communication skills	*integrity*
maturity	*intelligence*
enthusiasm	*willingness to take risks*
work experience	*self-confidence*

If your class is multilingual, compare the rankings of the different nationalities and cultures represented. In the original survey, conducted by an executive search company, communication skills were considered the most important factor.

DID YOU KNOW?

Give students time to read through all the facts in this section. Ask them to find:

- two facts that they consider most important for business people to know
- the most difficult to believe
- two facts they already knew.

The photo in the Student's Book shows a range of satellite dishes. Brainstorm with your class all the different ways of communicating, from formal letters to phone calls.

LANGUAGE WORK

Connected speech

1 Students read the information and look at the two soundwaves. They illustrate why spoken English is often so difficult – words merge into each other and sounds are changed or lost. The recorded messages in question 2, on the other hand, demonstrate how annoying and difficult it can be to follow spoken sentences if the words are clearly separated from each other and thus sound mechanical.

1 After students have done the matching exercise (Transcription **a** matches the soundwave on the left), ask students which sounds more natural. Even if students are not familiar with phonetics, the fact that /dʒəwɒnəgəʊnaʊ/ appears as one long mass, whereas /duː juː wɒnt tʊ gəʊ naʊ/ consists of short bursts, should make the difference clear. An explanation for transcription **a** is that when we start speaking, we place our mouths in the correct position to form the first sound, but our brain is already signalling to our mouths and vocal chords that they must prepare for the later sounds.

2 **5.1** Play the tape, stopping after each message.

1 an answering machine
2 the speaking clock
3 a computer voice message
4 directory enquiries
These messages follow pattern **b** (sandwave 1)

3 Class discussion. If you are working in a non-English-speaking country and have access to a phone during the lesson, you could try calling the speaking clock or other services to check out and compare the voice patterns.

② Students practise reading the sentences in pairs. You could ask them first to underline which syllables they think are stressed and cross out words or syllables that will disappear in connected speech.

5.2 Play the tape for students to listen to the sentences being spoken quickly. They can compare with their own version. You may like to play the tape again for choral or individual repetition of the sentences.

Reporting

Reported speech

Students read through the example sentences. You could ask them to say the sentences in direct speech to make sure everyone understands the tense and pronoun changes that take place in reported speech.

① Students do the matching exercise as instructed.

1 b	3 e	5 a
2 d	4 c	6 f

Go though page 169 in the Reference section if your students need more explanation of this point.

② Students could do this exercise in pairs. They should use the example sentences to help them and possibly put the verbs into sentences of their own, e.g.:

*He **admitted that** he had forgotten to send the report.*

*She **admits that** she should work harder.*
*They **admitted phoning** the States from the office!*

admit: 1, 3, 6	instruct: 3, 5
advise: 2, 3, 5	mention: 1, 3, 6
ask: 4, 5	promise: 1, 2, 4
assure: 2	persuade: 2, 5
explain: 1, 3	recommend: 1, 3, 6
hint: 1, 3	reply: 1, 3
inform: 2	urge: 5
insist: 1, 3	

③ Students do the exercise as instructed.

1 assured	4 urged
2 say	5 insisted
3 Tell	

You could ask students to rephrase the same sentences, if possible, using the alternative verb:
He replied that he had rescheduled …
Sentences 1, 3, 4, and 5 can be rephrased.

④ Students complete the sentences as instructed. Students should again refer to the Reference section if they have problems with tense changes.

2 She asked if we would like to branch out into a new sector.
3 He explained how to do it.
4 She informed us that she might not be able to make it to the meeting.
5 She told us we could do it quicker if we bypassed a few layers.
6 He wondered if we had noticed any potential threats.
7 She suggested that we should call for a taxi as it was getting late.

Point out that the modal verbs *could*, *might* and *should* didn't change (modal verbs are covered in Unit 12).

⑤ Chinese Whispers will be familiar to most people; the procedure given here prepares for the task which follows. If your class is large, divide into groups of five or six. If not, the game can be played with one small class. Allocate each student one letter from A to E. If you have access to another room, A and B students should remain in the room and the rest move to the other room.

Student A reads the story on page 147 of the Student's Book. He / she then repeats it quietly to Student B, who listens but does not comment. Student C is called into the room and Student A leaves. Student B repeats the story to Student C, and so on.

When everyone has been told the story, they all read the original version on page 147 and fill in the table in the Student's Book. The process of filling in the form will entail students using indirect speech, e.g.:

You said Thursday, not Tuesday.

Taking messages

① 5.3 Play each message once. Play the tape a second time, asking students to say *Stop!* and then to repeat the phrases which show the people calling haven't understood correctly. Go through other phrases they can use, such as:

Sorry, was that J or G?

I didn't quite catch that. Could you confirm that address by fax?

② You may need to play the tape again. Ask students to write out the whole message correctly.

Correct messages:
– Ring Mr Pieruccioni, SIAS Systems on 050–273734 before seven tonight. If not, he said he'd call you back on Thursday morning.
– Nicole Schulze wants a copy of the new catalogue. Please send to: 6 Von Melle Park, 3800 Wiesbaden, Germany.

③ Make sure students use phrases such as *new / next word, new / next line, capital C, small d, that's one word*, etc. You may want to review pronunciation of certain letters of the alphabet with your class, depending on their own language.

④ 5.4 Play the messages, repeating each one as many times as necessary to give students time to note down the information. Most answering machines retain messages, and even in our own language it is necessary to listen again to take in all the information. Students then write the messages using indirect speech. Ask individual students to read their messages. Correct using the tapescript.

Possible answers:
1 Jan Koopman from TCX called. He was given your name by Peter Jones, who said that you might have the address of the shipping agent in Tokyo. He asked if you could e-mail it to him. His address is jankoopman@hpstar.com.
2 Nate called to thank you for last Saturday. He suggested meeting next week.
3 Carl Hengersberg called with the sales figures he promised you. Fase Out providers have gone up by over 115% in the last year, and the new instant translators by about 60%. His telephone number is 0049–89–317–9500.

BUSINESS SKILLS

Communication tips

① Students do the exercise as instructed. Encourage them to suggest other tips.

Suggested answers (assuming that letters will be word-processed):
1 T5	5 E	8 T, L
2 L6	6 E	9 L, E, T
3 T7	7 T	10 L
4 E, L		

② Ask students if they can remember the first time they made a call in English. Did they feel nervous? Elicit the problems they encounter when calling in English.

1 Students can work in pairs or groups. Go through their list of rules. Then take them through the various stages of a typical phone call and find out which stages are difficult. If you think your students need more structure to

prepare for the role-play in the following exercise, copy this chart onto the board for them to follow.

A	B
Ask to speak to B.	Reply.
Announce who you are.	Respond. Ask how A is.
Respond. Initiate small talk.	Continue small talk.
Explain reason for call.	Make comment or ask question.
Respond and give details.	Check you've understood the details.
Confirm or clarify.	Respond.
Thank and say goodbye.	Say goodbye.

2 Students practise the preceding steps using the telephone role-plays in their book. Use real phones if possible. Do the exercise yourself with less confident students.

3 Again, draw on students' experience in letter-writing. Do they have a list of phrases they use regularly? Encourage them to make a note of phrases they read in letters they receive so as to be able to use them again. Explain that although letters are more formal than e-mail or faxes, they, too, have become more informal and that English business letters are generally quite concise. Explain that expressions such as *We would appreciate it if you could …* are being replaced more and more now by *Please could you … .*

You could brainstorm expressions used to open paragraphs when you want to thank, regret, inform, ask for information, enclose, and finish letters.

Go through the layout of the letter on page 148 of the Student's Book. Check that students know the pronunciation of *Mr* and *Ms*, and the difference between *Miss*, *Mrs*, and *Ms*. Point out that, when in doubt, *Ms* is preferable nowadays for a woman. Americans usually write a full stop after *Mr.*, *Mrs.*, and *Ms*.

Students can work in pairs to carry out one or more of the tasks. Allocate tasks which are appropriate to your students' needs. They can compare with other pairs. Correct together. Ask individual students to write up their e-mail, fax, or

voicemail message on the board, guided and corrected by the others.

Avoiding misunderstandings

1 Students read the text alone, using dictionaries if necessary. Tell students that the article represents a very stereotypical view of American behaviour designed to highlight possible mistakes – it should not be interpreted as being true of the majority of American business people.

1 You could ask students to find synonyms in English for the words, or translate them into their own language. You may wish to point out the American spelling of *humor*.

booming:	loud, resonant
reiterates:	repeats
disconcerting:	confusing
gregarious:	sociable
delegation:	group of representatives
camaraderie:	friendship

2 Students do the activity as instructed. (The mistakes are highlighted in the listening exercise which follows.)

2 [5.5] Play the tape.

1 Go through the mistakes she mentions and compare with students' views. Check answers in the tapescript; a summary is given below.

Suggested answers:
His speaks loudly and confidently, which would be interpreted as arrogance.
He sits at the head of the table, making him seem the sole decision-maker.
He stands up to make his opening remarks and only makes eye contact with the leader. This would be interpreted by the others as being looked down on.
He makes jokes, which do not translate well.
His informality would appear disrespectful.

He displays irritation, a sign of impatience, and
resents having to repeat himself, making no
concessions to his audience, whose native
language is not English.
He is uncomfortable with silence.
He misinterprets gestures such as nodding, which
means that they have understood, not
necessarily that they agree.

2 Discuss. Elicit misunderstandings arising not
only in meetings, but in other situations: small
talk, business lunches, giving and receiving gifts,
physical contact, etc.

3 Discuss. Draw on students' experience of
translators and interpreters. You could also
discuss the subject of sub-titles on films at the
cinema, translations of books, etc.

MEETINGS

Students read the two extracts, and the
instructions for the meeting. Help with any
difficulties students may have with the extracts.
The companies are both British: BT
(telecommunications) and NatWest (banking).

Put students into small groups to do steps 1–3.
Check that students are familiar with *yellow pages*
(a business telephone directory which lists
businesses by type. As in previous *Meetings*
sections, appoint one person to chair the
discussion and make sure that the points are
covered one by one; another should take notes.
Choose different students for these roles each time.
Ask students to take minutes, which can then form
a writing activity when the meeting is finished.

TABLE TALK

1 Students complete the quiz alone, then
compare answers. Students can compare their
answers with a partner, or you can organize a class
survey with one student writing the results on the
board. Let your students debate answers where
their opinions varied.

Discuss the impact of the Internet or mobile
phones in your students' countries.

Also ask them, which cultures or nationalities, in
their opinion, use gestures or 'touch' the most?

2 5.6 Play the tape once or twice. Discuss what
students know of aboriginal culture, and ask if they
were surprised by anything in the conversation.
Using the tapescript, check that students have not
missed anything.

If your class is multilingual, ask if there are
indigenous groups in your students' countries and
ask them to discuss their culture and how it differs
from the rest of the country.

If your students all come from the same country,
ask how culture varies from north to south, or east
to west, class to class, etc.

6 TRAVEL

WARM-UP

1 Top five travel fears

Ask students to work in pairs to discuss how often they travel abroad for work and what their five biggest fears are when travelling abroad . Discuss as a whole class.

2 Find the country

Ask students to draw the outlines of three individual countries on the board. They then have to guess each other's drawings and make comments on them, e.g. *You've drawn France too small, it's much bigger than Denmark*. They could then try to put a continent together. Students volunteer to add a country until a whole continent is drawn on the board. It would obviously be helpful to have a map of the world available. Somebody usually has one in an agenda or diary.

DID YOU KNOW?

Ask students not to look at the facts. Ask if they know the following:

- How long is the shortest regular scheduled flight?
- Where is the coldest inhabited place in the world?
- Which country has the highest car ownership?
- Which is the world's busiest airport?
- What is GMT?

Then give students one minute to find the answers to the above questions. This will encourage students to scan a text quickly for information without reading every word. After one minute, ask students to close their books, and elicit answers.

Next, open books again and give students one minute, alone, to prepare three more questions about the text.

Close books. Individual students ask their questions and the others volunteer answers.

Finally, open books and look for any facts that weren't covered in the previous two tasks. Discuss the facts that surprised or interested them most.

You may like to discuss the opening photo, and what students think it represents.

LANGUAGE WORK

Intonation

1 6.1 Students do the exercise as instructed. Play the tape completely first and ask students to fill in the answer.

Correct together. If answers vary, play parts of the tape again to decide who's right.

1	in a shop
2	at a train station
3	in a taxi
4	in a garage
5	at a hotel reception desk
6	in a restaurant

2 6.2 Ask students to read through the whole exercise first. Make sure everyone is familiar with the phrases used for requests. Then play the tape for students to proceed as instructed.

1 P	3 I	5 I	7 P	9 P
2 P	4 I	6 P	8 P	10 P

3 Students listen to sentences 1 and 2 again. Stop after each sentence and elicit the key word. The speaker's voice rises leading up to the key word. If you wish, you could continue listening to the remaining sentences.

1	States	6	exhaust and radiator
2	credit	7	thanks, would
3	take	8	tube
4	station	9	kind
5	cost	10	bill

4 Students read the dialogues twice, in pairs, changing roles. They should read all the dialogues politely.

travel, trip, journey

Point out to students that we don't say *a travel*, which is a common mistake. The word *travel* is an adjective as in *travel agent*, a verb as in *I travelled alone*, or a noun when used generally as in *Travel broadens the mind*. Note also the American spelling of *traveler, traveling*.

Students work alone then compare with a partner.

1	journey	6	trips
2	travel	7	journey
3	travel	8	travel
4	trip	9	travel
5	travel, travel	10	trip, trip

Students discuss their answers to the questions with a partner. You could ask individual students to present one of their answers to the rest of the class.

You may like to do some verb and adjective collocations of the words with your class, such as:

to go on a trip

to arrange a trip

a business trip

a pleasant trip

a tiring journey

Business trips

1 Students do the exercise as instructed. They can discuss the questions in groups if you have a large class. You could also discuss the secrets of Bill Gates' success, and whether the behaviour described in the article is typical of highly successful business people. You could also compare this article with the one on page 65 of the Student's Book, about another successful entrepreneur.

2 **6.3** Play the tape. Before students write a summary of what they've heard, you could ask some comprehension questions about the following points:

– How does Gates prepare for trips abroad? *(by reading books and articles on the places that have been recommended by the heads of Microsoft's local subsidiaries, both before he leaves and while travelling)*

– Where does his information come from? *(asking questions about the culture, ranging from history to art to local politics)*

– Give an example of how he uses the information. *(in product development, e.g. localizing products to cater for the high number of languages spoken in India / recruiting local talent / using information gathered in one country to apply to others)*

– What does 20% refer to? *(20% of what customers say is new and different from what others have said)*

– How does he travel (economy, club, etc.)? *(he usually travels Economy (UK; US Commercial) but on this occasion travelled Business Class)*

Intentions
Future continuous vs future simple

This section focuses on the use of the future continuous for actions that are part of the normal course of events, e.g. *I'll be seeing her tonight anyway, so I can give her your message then*. It does not cover actions that will be happening at a certain time in the future, e.g. *This time next month, I will be lying on the beach*. This is covered in Unit 7.

If students ask, you could explain that there is very little difference in meaning between: *I'm seeing her tonight, I'm going to see her tonight* and *I'll be seeing her tonight*, but that *I'll see her tonight* wouldn't be used in this sentence as it implies that the decision to meet her was made at the time of speaking.

Students read through the example sentences alone.

1 Students do the exercise as instructed.

Affirmative: underline <u>simple</u> in the first rule, <u>continuous</u> in the second.

Negative: underline <u>continuous</u> in the first rule, <u>simple</u> in the second.

Interrogative: underline <u>simple</u> in the first rule, <u>continuous</u> in the second.

② Students do the exercise as instructed.

> 1 will be arriving
> 2 Will you be paying
> 3 will be speaking, will give
> 4 will be checking in
> 5 Will you help
> 6 I will not be going

③ Elicit from students: the present continuous and the future *going to*. These are quite similar in use to the future continuous, but not to the future simple. Go through the Reference section, page 157.

BUSINESS SKILLS

Travel survival kit

There are four activities in this section. If time is short, choose those that your students need most, and come back to the others at a later date.

When doing the role-play activities, ask students to do them a second time (swapping roles, and with a different partner), as students faced with these situations will mostly be the customer and not the travel agent, shop assistant, etc.

① **Giving directions**

Check that students understand all of the expressions, particularly the use of the verbs with prepositions: *get to*, *turn off*, *stay in*, *go straight on*, *head southwards*, etc. Brainstorm other verbs used for giving directions.

1 6.4 Introduce the listening activity by explaining that often when you're listening, you don't have a map to follow. Play the tape for students to do the exercise as instructed. The answer is on page 150 of the Student's Book.

2 Students work in pairs. They shouldn't give the destination before starting their directions.

You could also do this activity yourself with the whole class. Give students a starting point then take them all over town before arriving at the destination you've chosen. Find out how many get there!

② **Car rental**

Students read through the expressions. Check that everyone understands all the terms used in car rental concerning papers and insurance.

Students work in pairs and do the role-play as instructed.

③ **Checking into a hotel**

After students have read through the expressions, you could brainstorm all the facilities and services you find in hotels and hotel rooms. What goes wrong when you stay in hotels? Go through some expressions for dealing with problems, e.g.:

I don't have any towels.

The tap's dripping.

I asked for a wake-up call at 7.30.

I can't turn the radiator down.

Students do the role-play as instructed.

④ **Changing a flight reservation**

Students read the expressions and then do the role-play as instructed. If possible use real phones if you have a phone in the classroom. You may want to add some other role-plays. You could bring some travel brochures into class, even if they're not in English, and ask students to role-play a travel agent and customer going through the different choices when booking a trip. The longest part of booking a trip is often going through the possibilities.

The worst trip ever ...

Give students time to read through the instructions and have a look at the board game. Make sure everyone understands *toss a coin*, *heads*, and *tails*! Students take turns to toss the coin.

The length of their dialogues will obviously depend on the situation they find themselves in, so point out that some of the dialogues only have to be short. However, make sure everyone uses expressions for attracting attention, interrupting, requesting, apologizing, thanking, replying to thanks, etc. Each dialogue should begin with some sort of expression and not just go straight into the subject itself. You could do a demonstration dialogue with a more confident student first, as an example.

Monitor progress, listening in and offering help when necessary. Make a note of mistakes, good expressions you heard, wrong expressions, problems of intonation, and correct after the activity is finished.

MEETINGS

Before beginning the exercise, establish where the next Summer and Winter Olympics are being held, and whether the dates for the following Olympics have been decided. Tell students that their town, or capital, or the town where your course is taking place wants to make a bid for those Olympics. Students can decide whether they should be Summer or Winter Olympics. Give students enough time to read the statistics as these should help them to some extent to establish costs.

1   Divide the class into two committees of three or four students. If your class is too small, or numbers don't match, students can double up roles. Appoint one person as leader of the meeting, another can take notes.

2   Put the two committees together to discuss the result of their meetings and to answer the other questions.

As an extra writing activity, students could present a written report of their arguments for their decision.

TABLE TALK

1   Students complete the quiz alone, then compare and discuss their answers with a partner. Students may think of other answers to these questions. Elicit them at the end of the activity and discuss with the rest of the class.

2   Ask students to prepare about six to eight questions alone. Don't give any suggestions at this point.

1   6.5   Play the tape. Students check their questions with the ones they think were asked on the tape. Play the tape again, pausing between each speaker, and ask students to formulate the question that was asked.

Possible questions:

1   How many days annual leave are you entitled to?
2   How far ahead do you plan your holidays?
3   Do you keep in touch with your office?
4   Do you generally do what you want to do on holiday?
5   What are the popular holiday destinations for people in your country?
6   Are there any places you would avoid on holiday?

2   In pairs, students ask and answer each others' questions. You could ask individual students to volunteer to make a short presentation about their own holiday, or their partner's, in front of the rest of the class.

7 PLANNING

WARM-UP

1 Predictions and forecasts

Ask students if they think it is possible to make 15- or 20-year business plans. What about 10- or 5-year plans? Does the size or type of company influence how far ahead it can realistically plan? Has their company ever had to completely abandon its plans after forecasts proved to be incorrect?

Then ask students if they know of any wildly wrong predictions and forecasts that have been made in the business world and use this as a lead into the *Did You Know?* section.

2 Short-term and long-term plans

Find out from students what the word *planning* means to them both on a day-to-day or short-term basis, and long-term. What sort of short- or long-term plans are they involved in? Elicit everything, from arranging a meeting the following Friday, to planning the launch of a product in five years.

DID YOU KNOW?

The illustration shows one of Leonardo da Vinci's sketches. Can students think of any other inventors who were ahead of their time?

Students read through the facts. Ask them which they think are the two most incredible predictions in the list. Then ask why people make predictions which are so wildly wrong. Can they think of any others, such as business or political predictions, that have been made in their country?

You could use these sentences to check students' use of indirect speech (see Unit 5).

LANGUAGE WORK

Pronunciation

1 This exercise practises the difference between /r/ and /l/ in initial and final positions, and before consonants. Many nationalities experience problems in at least one of these areas. You should

say each pair of words yourself first, then ask students to repeat in chorus or individually.

2 [7.1] Students do the exercise as instructed. Play the tape once or twice. Correct together.

1 I'll	5 world
2 They'll	6 bolt
3 rebid	7 filed
4 light	8 wrong

You could play the tape again for repetition of the words within the sentences.

3 Students say the words to themselves.

fired and *filed* are one-syllable words. The only words in the exercise with an extra syllable in the past simple are *forwarded* and *interested*.

Looking ahead

Future perfect and future continuous

This section introduces the future perfect plus further uses of the future continuous (see Unit 6). Students read through the example sentences. Make sure everyone is familiar with the grammatical structure of these tenses: *will have* + past participle, and *will be* + present participle.

1 Students can discuss the answers to the questions with a partner. Correct together.

1 a. In b the speaker is making a request.
2 c next March.
d ... and then I'll move on.
3 e
4 g ... so don't ring me then.
h ... when I get to the hotel.

2 Students do the exercise as instructed.

1 will have diversified, will rise / will have risen
2 will be, will be lying
3 will have been
4 will you have already gone?
5 will have completed, will be celebrating
6 will be having
7 will have / will have had
8 will you let

After students have finished the exercise, focus on sentence 8 (... *when you have come to a decision*) and remind them that we use the present perfect rather than the future perfect in temporal clauses (i.e. after *if*, *when*, *as soon as*, *until*, etc.).

③ **7.2** First, students focus on the illustration. Then, discuss questions 1–4 either in groups if your class is big, or class as a whole. The illustration was drawn in 1939.
Students listen to the tape and make notes. Compare with what they predicted themselves.

World population:	up by 20% to 8 billion.
Crime:	two different opinions are given: the first speaker thinks crime rates will come down, the second speaker thinks security will be a growing profession
Leisure time:	will increase
Age of retirement:	will increase to at least 70
Biggest shortages of natural resources:	water
Format of books:	electronic
Price of electronic goods:	will drop by up to 80%
Most needed professions:	entertainment, sports, nursing, and security

Probability and possibility

① Students work in pairs and mark a percentage against each phrase. Tell them that they can write an approximate percentage too, such as 20–30%. Point out that the intonation used in the phrases can sometimes increase or decrease the probability.

Percentages will vary, but the suggested order from most sure to least sure is
6–2–4–9–8–5–3–7–10–11.

Ask students to underline the words or phrases in these sentences that indicate certainty, probability and improbability, i.e. *absolutely certain*, *bound to*, *should / ought to*, *no chance of ...* .

② Students work alone or in pairs to do this exercise. They can choose all or some of the events. They then compare with a partner / another pair.

③ Students complete the quiz alone, then compare with a partner.

Using *may*, *can*, and some of the words and phrases in exercise 1, ask students to give other predictions of events that are certain, likely or unlikely to happen to them, their companies, families, etc., in the future.

BUSINESS SKILLS

Making arrangements

① Students read through the expressions alone.
1 As instructed, students insert the appropriate title for each set of expressions.

Order of headings:
Opening
Suggesting
Offering
Changing
Confirming

2 **7.3** Play the tape once and ask students to tell you when the two men will actually meet. Play the tape a second time and ask them to note down why they can't meet at the other times mentioned. You could write up a list of dates on the board going from Wednesday 23rd to Thursday 31st, and ask them which ones were discussed, and why, during the two phone calls.

Conversation 1:	
Wednesday 23rd	Firman is busy at the warehouse all day.
Thursday 24th	Firman is in the lab all day
Friday 25th	Palmieri is going to Paris for a long weekend.
Tuesday 29th	meeting arranged for 10.30.
Conversation 2:	
Thursday 31st	meeting re-arranged for 2.30. They are going to meet for lunch at 1.00.

3 Role-play. Students follow their instructions on pages 137 and 143. Remind them to include all the 'hellos', small talk, etc., that they learned in Unit 5.

2 Writing activity. Allow students time to read the e-mail and to write their reply.

> **Possible reply:**
>
> Thank you for your message regarding our meeting next week. I'm really sorry, but something unexpected has cropped up in our plant in Romania and I will be away until next Friday. Would the following Monday at the same time suit you? I'm terribly sorry about this as I realize you will have to change your flight arrangements. I will certainly send you the agenda for the meeting and I look forward to seeing you a week on Monday.
> Best regards,
>   (first name)

As an extra writing activity, you could ask students to write Ms Smith's reply, either confirming the new date, or suggesting yet another date.

You could also turn this into another telephone role-play in which case Ms Smith is not free the following Monday and students have to find a new date.

Planning a project

1 Students do the exercise as instructed.

1 g, i	4 d, g	7 i
2 a	5 a, b, c	8 d
3 h, i	6 b	9 b, e, g

If your students all work for the same company, ask them to work in groups. If not, they can work in pairs and compare. Ask individual students to volunteer to give a presentation about planning a project in their company.

2 The concept of project management developed out of the need to make the best use of available resources, and has its origins in the American space programme in the 1960s. The diagram shows the two most widely used methods of critical path analysis, which represent the stages of a project and the time allowed for their completion.

Other project plans might be:
- consumer analysis, e.g. what is the need for the product / service?
- market analysis
- competitive analysis (i.e. SWOT – see Unit 3)
- distribution analysis.

On the basis of these analyses, detailed forecasts and plans can then be made.

3 Using the diagrams in exercise 2 as models, students complete this exercise and compare with a partner. If your students' jobs do not involve planning projects, you could let them illustrate the planning of a personal or home project they are working on.

Planning an empire

Elicit names famous in the business world with your students. Brainstorm the secrets to their success. Discuss how some business people become better known to the public than others; because of the product they have launched, or because of their personality?

Students read the profile of Richard Branson. They should use dictionaries if available for the meaning of the words in italics and other new vocabulary.

daring exploits:	potentially dangerous activities
in the throes of change:	changing with difficulty
peers:	contemporaries
unabashed enthusiasm:	eagerness which is obvious to everyone

Ask students what they already knew about Richard Branson and the Virgin empire, and what they learned from the article.

1–**3** Students discuss the questions in small groups, or as a whole class. Ask what sort of qualities and characteristics Richard Branson has that other business people don't. How does he compare to their CEOs?

Ask students to give examples of their companies' *webs of interest*. Discuss any disadvantages of a company being associated primarily with its leader.

As a writing activity, you could ask your class to imagine that they have to write a similar magazine article about their CEO or Managing Director.

MEETINGS

First, give students time to read through the introduction and instructions for this meeting.

1 Organize your class into groups of three. Make sure they don't all choose the same Virgin product. You can double up roles if you don't have exact groups of three.

With small classes, this can be carried out as either a group discussion or debate of one or more or the Virgin products. The products / services of the subsidiaries shown are: financial planning, holidays, soft drinks, air travel, music, and cosmetics.

2 Students form new groups as instructed. They should draw up their plan of action in writing, following the project-planning steps introduced on page 63 of the Student's Book.

TABLE TALK

1 Focus attention on the photo, which shows transgenic mice. They have been injected with a jellyfish GFP (green fluorescent protein) gene that causes the skin to glow green under blue light, and is used in cancer research. Elicit other experiments in genetic engineering which have been in the news recently. Ask for your students' reactions to these experiments.

7.4 Play the tape once or twice for students to list the main activities. You may prefer to dictate your own comprehension questions:

– Which speaker is very against genetic engineering and cloning? *(B)*

– How did many people react to the first heart transplant? *(they thought it was unnatural and wrong)*

– Why does the second speaker say that cloning is different? *(she regards it as ethically unacceptable)*

– What examples do the speakers give of things that could be done through cloning, to animals, and to people? *(farming of babies or brains)*

– What are their arguments for genetic testing? *(eliminating violence, early diagnosis of illness)*

For further discussion: In 1998 the European Parliament approved the patenting of genetically-modified plants and animals, but not of humans. It explicitly banned the cloning of human beings and changing human genes in such a way that could be inherited. Ask for students' opinions on how much governments should intervene in scientific progress.

2 Students work alone to decide how likely it is that each of the activities will become everyday reality. They compare their ideas in groups.

8 PRODUCTS

WARM-UP

1 Recycling

Ask students to do the warm-up activity on photocopiable page 75 of this book. For durations of over 20 years, consider answers correct if they are within five years, the other durations within one year.

How many years products last		How many years rubbish lasts	
audio cassette	100	aluminium can	80–100
freezer	20	leather footwear	50
sweater	5	nuclear waste	24,400
telephone	25	orange peel	up to 0.5
televisions	12	plastic bag	10–20
violin	350 +	plastic jar / bottle	50–80
white lines on road	3	wool socks	1–5

You could give an added dimension by asking students to bet on their estimations. For example, for each estimate they bet between $1 and $10 – the more they bet, the more certain they are that their estimate is correct. Then you can find out who has won and lost most.

You could discuss the products in the illustration, and how long they are likely to last.

2 Product materials

Give each student a picture of some kind of tool or other product (which may or may not be pertinent to their field of business). These can be found in magazines, or DIY catalogues and publicity. In pairs, students question their partner to find out what the object is, by asking questions such as:

Is it made of X?

Is it used for Y?

Questions must be formulated so that a *Yes / No* answer can be given. You may want to review vocabulary for different materials: *metal*, *steel*, *wool*, *glass*, *rubber*, etc. Also, shapes and sizes: *round*, *square*, *hollow*, *thick*, *thin*, etc.

DID YOU KNOW?

Give students one minute to read the facts very quickly, then close their books. Ask them how many brand names or products they can remember, how many company names, and how many countries were mentioned. Open books and check together. Ask students if the product(s) their company makes has to be adapted for the foreign market? Does the name have to be changed to avoid pronunciation difficulties? Are there counterfeit versions of any of their products?

Ask students how market research is carried out in their company. Which brand names have entered into their language?

LANGUAGE WORK

Word stress: noun vs verb

1 8.1 Play the tape while students fill in the table. You could ask students to repeat the words after the speakers on the tape.

verb	stress	vowel	stress + vowel	no difference
command				✓
estimate		✓		
graduate		✓		
import	✓			
object	✓			
process				✓*
produce			✓	
record	✓			
reject	✓			
support				✓

*to pro'cess has a different meaning (to take part in a procession).

2 Students do the exercise as instructed. Not all speakers of English will agree on the exact pronunciation of some of the words. As a general rule, two-syllable words have the stress on the initial syllable if they are nouns, and on the second if they are verbs.

Pronunciation of *w*

1 First, go through some words containing *w* with your class. Write up on the board: *who, when, way, wrist, blown, saw.* Ask individual students to tell you what happens to the *w* in these words.

8.2 Students mark the words containing the sound /w/ and then listen to the tape to check their answers.

were	would
which	wood

2 **8.3** Students do the exercise as instructed.

1 verse	4 bolts
2 vote's	5 west
3 few	6 bat

If students need further practice distinguishing initial /b/ and /f/, and /v/ and /w/, then write the words below on the board. The words in each line all rhyme with each other, the only difference is in the initial consonant. Tell students to take it in turns to read the words at random – their partner will say if it's A, B, C, or D. Do a few first yourself with the whole class.

A	B	C	D
bile	file	vile	while
bowl	foal	vole	whole
burst	first	versed	worst
buyer	fire	via	wire

Future products

The passive

Students read through all the example sentences alone.

1 Students answer questions 1–3.

1 Sentences **b**, **c**, **f**, and **g** are passive. The verb *to be* is used with the past participle.
2 The passive is used when the agent is of no interest or unknown.
3 **b** The government is raising taxes.
  c They stop the machine once a week.
  f Somebody left the computer on all night.

In these three sentences, we need to add an agent, i.e. the person or thing carrying out the action.

Remind students of the passive *to be born* in English.

Also, the use of *It is said, supposed, thought, believed, assumed, rumoured … .* For example, *It is said that he's the richest man in the company.*

Students should refer to page 163 in the Reference section for more information about the passive.

2 Students do the exercise as instructed. Ask them to say which sentences are passive.

1 had	4 have
2 has	5 is reduced
3 was	

3 Students do the exercise as instructed.

1 may have been found
2 could be recognized, had still not been found
3 are being made
4 will never be totally controlled
5 has been put back
6 should have been completed, has been delayed, will now be completed
7 are being carried out
8 is not usually delivered, may not have received

4 Give students time to read through the table. They should use dictionaries or ask you for the meaning of new vocabulary.

Then, students discuss the answers to questions 1–3 with a partner, and compare with other pairs.

Sequences

Students study the example sentences alone. Elicit any other sequencing words they know: *first of all, next, afterwards, eventually* (a false friend in Latin languages), *so, thus, consequently*, etc.

1 Students do the exercise as instructed. If your students work in the software industry, the ordering task should be straightforward, and you could ask students to describe each stage before linking them as instructed. If students from other professional areas find the task challenging, you could provide the order suggested below to allow them to concentrate directly on the sequencing task; then focus on those stages which apply to their own field.

A typical sequence would be:
1   requirements analysis
2   specifications
3   technical design
4   development
5   testing
6   installation
7   quality assurance (this is likely to continue throughout the life cycle)
8   training
9   maintenance
10 new release

2 Students do the exercise as instructed. The associations students make will to some extent be determined by their product / service. Here is a rough guide. Numbers refer to the sequence in exercise 1.

assessment	1, 5	error detection	3, 4, 5, 7
benchmarking	5	feasibility	1, 2
budget	1, 2	feedback	5, 6
constraints	2	guarantee	9
control	5, 7	monitoring	5, 7
definition	2	repair	7, 9
delivery	6	research	1
distribution	6, 10	solution	3

3 Students work in pairs or small groups to describe the life cycle of their own product or service. Encourage students to explain how the system is set up, organized, focused, and manned. They should go through each individual stage. For example, in a manufacturing industry, the start of the cycle could be when the customer order is received and how it is subsequently scheduled, then how raw materials are ordered and received, followed by how production on the order or batch is initiated. The end of the cycle might be how the order is shipped and subsequently received by the customer.

BUSINESS SKILLS

Selling your product

Ask students to choose a product from the photos in the Student's Book. Before beginning the exercise you could review the vocabulary covered in the warm-up activity for describing objects. The easiest way to do this is to take an object yourself and describe it, deliberately using as many different expressions as you can, and giving students time to note each one. Take the top of your marker pen, for example, and say:

This looks a bit like the top of something, it appears to be made of some sort of plastic, it's about two centimetres long, it could be used for protecting a pen.

Students then proceed with one or other of these exercises as instructed. Depending on class size, students could work in teams to prepare a joint presentation of their group of products.

1 The focus here is on using ingenuity to imagine what the product might be used for and then describe it using the language they have practised.

a Portable Stoplight, which allows pedestrians
to stop traffic away from official crossings
b 360° Panorama Camera, to take all-round
photographs simultaneously
c Self-cooling Hat, with a fan which pumps out
hot air from inside the hat to keep the wearer
cool

1	D
2	E
3	C
4–5	F
6–8	B
9	A

Possible summary:
Magazines and catalogues arrive by truck at the
recycling plant, where they are lifted by a forklift
truck onto a conveyor belt. The belt carries them
across a sorting area where contaminants such as
plastic bags are removed by hand, and on to a
baler which compacts the paper into a tight
bundle and binds it with wire. This is transported
to the de-inking plant, where the baling wires are
cut and loose magazines released onto a
conveyor. The magazines are carried to a pulper
which stirs the paper with water until a thin pulp
is formed. This then runs through a series of
purifying steps to remove other contaminants
such as glues and non-paper inserts, and is piped
to the paper machine. Through a series of
drainage stages, pressure rolls and dryer rolls, the
pulp is turned into paper and wound onto huge
rolls. Later it is cut to size.

2 The products themselves will be familiar; students should focus on how to make them seem different and better than competing products. If they work for a manufacturing company with a product which competes with one of those shown, they may prefer to substitute their own!

3 Students work in pairs. They should point out the 'merits' of their object, and mention value for money, quality, and how useful or attractive their product is. Alternatively, you could have a group discussion as to the sales potential of the various products and decide which ones are worth promoting.

Processes

1   1 Before students look at the diagram, ask them to discuss what problems they think are involved in recycling colour and glossy paper – from when the collection trucks deliver the magazines and catalogues to the materials-processing facility, to when the final product comes out of the paper-making machines. Ask them to suggest what contaminants will need removing; this will enable you to teach useful vocabulary which they will need for the listening; *plastic grocery bags*, *glues*, *non-paper inserts*, and *staple wire* are all mentioned, but you could add others.

2–3 [8.4] Play the tape for students to do the activity as instructed. With less able students, ask them to read the tapescript before writing their description. Remind students that active verbs generally make what you say more dynamic, and ask them to balance the number of active and passive verbs that they use.

2 Students do the exercise as instructed. As an alternative, students could explain to their partner how to do one of the following: get residence or a driving licence in their country, send an e-mail, use a public phone, programme a VCR, find information on the Internet, etc.

You could also ask them to draw something and explain how it works, for example a redesigned human body, a housework robot, or a machine for testing intelligence.

Life cycle

Students read the introduction to this section. Discuss.

1   Students can work alone or in pairs. They should compare their answers with other students. Go through any answers which were very different from the rest of the class and discuss.

2   Class discussion. If your students come from different countries, ask them to compare how school subjects are taught. Brainstorm ideas for teaching other school subjects differently.

MEETINGS

Students should read through the whole section and follow the stages as instructed. The procedure given is suitable for a formal meeting; if you have a small group you may prefer to conduct this as a discussion activity. In this case stage 1 could become a simple summarizing task of the three texts. Stage 2 describes the 'marketing mix'; students' views will probably depend on which stage of the process they themselves are involved in. In stage 5, other ways might be:

– creating an advertising gimmick closely associated with the product / service (such as a character who uses it and who appears across an entire advertising campaign)

– associating the product / service with a good quality of life.

TABLE TALK

1   Students discuss their answer to the first quiz question in pairs. Before listening to the tape, brainstorm students for a list of questions that could be used to find out whether someone is influenced or not by advertising.

8.5   Play the tape once. Students decide which person's view came closest to their own. Play the tape again. Elicit from students the various questions the man asked to find out whether the woman was influenced by advertising. Ask how they would have answered those questions.

2   Allow students time to read through the whole quiz and complete it. They can compare their answers in groups. Ask individual students to explain or justify their answers if they are very different from the others'.

As a follow up, you could ask your students how much they are affected by *warning adverts* as described by the woman in **8.5** , i.e. those which suggest lifestyle changes or appeal for charity funding. Students discuss to what extent adverts influence their decision to buy a product or defend a cause.

9 VISITING

WARM-UP

1 Exploring new countries

In groups, ask students to write down a list of two or three things that surprised them most when they visited a particular country (if possible, an English-speaking one). Discuss together, or in groups if you have a large class.

2 Cultures (for mixed-nationality classes)

Put students in groups with different nationalities. Each person writes down some facts about his / her country's traditions and customs. However some of the 'facts' must be false! They then read out their facts to each other, and the other students in their group have to guess whether they are true or false.

Find one or two original examples for your own country. If you are a British teacher, you could say, for example: *In Britain people start queuing outside Harrod's the night before the January sales start; In British pubs, waiters take your order and serve you.*

3 Cultures (for same nationality classes)

Students discuss in which countries (or towns in their own country) they have felt most / least at home and most / least like visitors. Discuss whether this was because the culture was very similar / different, or whether they were made to feel welcome / unwelcome.

DID YOU KNOW?

Students read through all the facts. Tell them to ask each other questions on how they behave with respect to some of the facts mentioned, e.g. punctuality, connotations of giving gifts, tipping, etc.

Ask students to imagine that their company is sending them on a six-month business secondment to another country. Students choose which country they would prefer to be sent to and discuss their choices in small groups, or class as a whole.

LANGUAGE WORK

American and British accents

1 **9.1** Students read the whole exercise before you play the tape. Play the tape once or twice. Correct together. Point out to students that this exercise is to increase their awareness of different accents, but that they should use the pronunciation that sounds most natural to them, or the one they're used to saying, and not try and force the occasional American or British sound into the way they already speak.

adult: S	lever: V	tomato: C, V
clerk: V	metal: C	Tuesday: V
garage: S	nuclear: V	twenty: C
herb: C	path: V	vase: V
leisure: V	privacy: V	vitamin: C, V

You could play the tape once more, pausing after each pair of words, and ask individual students to repeat the word they feel is most natural to them.

2 Students discuss the questions in small groups, or class as a whole.

3 Discuss the question as instructed. If your students all come from the same country, ask them if they can give you examples of regional accents and dialects. You may need to exercise care with this question, especially if you have students from different parts of the same country, as regional accents can be a sensitive issue.

Pronunciation of *th*

1 Say the words *think* and *those* very clearly to your students before they complete the exercise. Students will probably need to say the words aloud to themselves to find the answers. Correct after exercise 2.

2 **9.2** Play the tape once, then a second time, pausing after each word for correction and repetition.

thank: /θ/	clothes: /ð/
therefore: /ð/	enthusiasm: /θ/
thorough: /θ/	sunbathe: /ð/
growth: /θ/	smooth: /ð/
worth: /θ/	

Welcoming visitors

①   Students do the exercise as instructed. Ask them to cover exercise 2.

②   Students do the matching exercise. You will need to check students' answers to exercise 1. They may not have written the same replies, but their versions could be perfectly correct!

You could ask students to work in pairs. Student A asks questions from the first exercise to Student B who has to react as quickly as possible with the right response from the second exercise.

You could also ask students to change the replies to the questions in the first exercise, e.g.:

A: *Have you been waiting long?*

B: *No not long. The plane was early, but it gave me time to change some currency.*

a 2	c 2	e 3	g 5	i 1
b 1	d 4	f 5	h 7	j 6

③   Students do the exercise as instructed. Encourage them to use or adapt questions and answers from the previous two exercises. Ask pairs to volunteer to do their role-play in front of the rest of the class.

④   ☐9.3☐   Allow students time to prepare their questions alone. Play the tape once through completely. Play it a second time, pausing after each question to allow students to compare their questions with those on the tape.

signing the register:	*Would you mind just signing the register?*
offering coffee:	*Can I get you a coffee while you're waiting?*
asking about his flight:	*So, did you have a good flight here?*

asking him to follow her:	Will you follow me please, and I'll take you up.
warning him about the floor:	Oh, by the way, mind the floors. They've just been polished and they're still a bit slippery.

⑤   Students do the role-play as instructed. Ask them to do the role-play a second time with another partner, swapping roles.

Local knowledge

Students work in pairs or groups. If necessary, find an atlas, or ask students to use world maps in their pocket diaries.

Note: The spellings of those names in languages which do not use the Roman alphabet vary from one source to another. Sources vary also on the lengths of rivers and heights of mountains.

See page 150 in the Student's Book for the answers to this section.

Students might like to discuss any re-naming of cities / regions in their own country's recent history, and why (naming after famous people, regional government reorganization, etc.).

Getting around
Infinitive vs gerund

①   Students read all the example sentences and then answer the questions.

1   **b**, **d**, **e**, **g**, and **i** are talking about an objective. The verb is acting like a noun in sentences **a**, **c**, **f**, **h**, and **j**.

2   *hate*, *love*, and *prefer* behave in the same way as *like*. *Enjoy* isn't used with the conditional in this way, but *I'd enjoy* + gerund is acceptable.

3   The infinitive is *to stop*. In **g**, the infinitive is used because we are talking about the objective, the reason for stopping. In **h**, the gerund *looking* is used to say that the activity is finished.

4   **h**, **g**

5   **i** is in the future (**j** is in the past).

Go through page 158 in the Reference section if your students would like to review the use of the gerund. You could ask students to give further examples of the gerund or infinitive after the verbs *stop* and *remember*.

2 Students do the exercise as instructed.

1 to get	6 thinking
2 Driving	7 to visit
3 to buy	8 going
4 stopping	9 to change
5 to have	10 writing

BUSINESS SKILLS

Visiting a factory

Students focus on the photos.

1 **9.4** The recording consists of eight extracts from a factory tour. Play the tape through without stopping and ask some gist questions. You may wish to pre-teach some vocabulary based on the tapescript, for example *spillaging (spilling)*, *jetty*, *state of the art*, *assembly line*, *welding*. Then play again, stopping after each extract for students to do the matching activity.

a 1	c 7	e 8	g 6
b 4	d 5	f 2	h 3

2 Discussion in groups, or class as a whole. If your students work directly in factories, or closely with the factories of their company, draw on their personal experience and knowledge.

3 Students do the exercise as instructed. Ask them to talk about the functions carried out in each part of their factory or office, who is in charge of them, how many people work in each part, the importance of each function, etc.

Visiting abroad

Students read the text. They should check the words and phrases in italics, using dictionaries, or asking you for the meaning.

canvassed:	invited by asking a large number of companies
submit:	offer for consideration
narrowing the field:	reducing the number of applicants by rejecting some
candidates:	applicants
mix-up:	confused situation
double-check:	make sure everything is correct
apologies:	expressions of regret
appointed time:	arranged meeting time

1 Ask some comprehension questions to make sure students understand the problem:

– Why did the Thai government agency contact the American engineering firms?
– Were there only four candidates?
– How many firms did the Thai delegation want to interview in Chicago?
– Why were the Thais not met at the airport?
– What arrangement was made for the following day?
– What happened? (ask students to look at the cartoon)

2 Then get feedback from students as to what happened. Tell the rest of the story:

> Finally, in mid-afternoon, he received a phone call from the visitors saying, 'We have been waiting at our hotel. No one has come to pick us up. We are simply not accustomed to this type of treatment. We have booked a flight out this afternoon to our next destination. Goodbye!'

Next, ask students what measures they take to welcome their guests, and how they themselves like to be welcomed when they travel abroad. Finally, they could think of improvements to the way their company presents itself and how it receives visitors, callers, and customers.

Sightseeing at home

Students do the exercise as instructed. If they live in the same town, they should compare and justify their choices. If they all come from different towns, encourage students to discuss the good and bad points of the places they have listed, and to recommend one or two places. You could use the exercise to review comparatives and superlatives: *the priciest restaurant*, *Nightclub X is more exclusive than Nightclub Y*, etc.

Sightseeing abroad

1 Students focus on the photos and identify them.

1 The photos depict Sydney Harbour Bridge, the Monorail, Darling Harbour, the Botanic Gardens, Chinatown, the Opera House. You could ask students to imagine that their business visitor is coming with his / her spouse and three children. Which activities would then become appropriate?

Answers will vary, but the following arise from the photographs:
- a boat trip around Darling Harbour
- a walk Sidney Harbour Bridge
- a trip on the Monorail
- a Chinese meal
- an evening stroll around Chinatown
- a night at the Opera
- a tour of the Opera House
- a visit to the Botanical Gardens

2 Students do the exercise as instructed. This can be a class discussion, or students can work in groups if you have a large class. As a follow up, ask students how much sightseeing they manage to do when on business trips. Do they have time to visit places?

2 Class discussion, or in groups or pairs. Students can choose one specific country, if they prefer, for the list of aspects in the Student's Book. They then compare with their own country.

If your class is multinational, put students from different countries in pairs and ask them to compare these aspects.

MEETINGS

Students read through the whole section alone. Make sure everyone understands the object of the meeting. Organize your class into groups. One person should chair the meeting and another take notes. Roles should be allocated to other members of the group. One person can be in charge of accommodation, meals, and transport; another in charge of the agenda, etc. However, the whole group should discuss each factor in the list.

If your class all come from the same town, they should use real places and people.

If your students are from different countries, they should either invent the town, or use the town where the English course is taking place.

When students have finished organizing the convention, ask them to use their notes and prepare a presentation to be presented by one member of each group in front of the rest of the class.

Let students decide whose convention would be the best organized!

As a writing activity, you could ask your class to present a written agenda of the convention to be sent to the sales staff of all branches of the company.

TABLE TALK

1 Ask students to concentrate on the photo and encourage them to speculate on what might be happening. Ask questions to focus their thoughts, e.g.:
- Why are the men in the cage?
- Did they volunteer to go in or were they paid?
- Why is there a chicken sitting on top of the cage?

Accept all suggestions as to what might be happening and let students agree or disagree. Reassure students that there is a true story behind the photo!

2 If you think your students will be able to follow the listening activity without this

preparatory exercise, you could go straight to exercise 3. Otherwise, go through the words. In groups, they should try to piece together the story. When they have finished, ask one student from each group to tell their group's version and see if the others agree or not. Don't tell students the real story at this point.

3 **9.5** Play the tape twice. First, ask your class to listen for the questions the listeners ask. Point out their informality, e.g. *What, in a cage?*

Then ask students to give the answers to these questions.

Play the tape once more for students who hadn't understood some of the questions or answers, pausing where necessary. Check how much of the story they had already guessed, or which groups were correct if you did exercise 2.

Possible summary using the words in exercise 2:

As a promotional stunt, the author of a book of vegetarian recipes offered to pay four men to live like battery hens for a week. They had a legal contract defining the conditions. They were barefoot in a wire cage and were fed through a tube. An audiotape played constant loud noises to simulate the conditions that hens live in.

Ask students if they would have bought the book as a result of this promotional stunt, and whether it was an effective way of promoting public awareness of the plight of some animals. Brainstorm ways of doing promotional stunts (serious or funny) for their own company. If your students work in a very large company, how do they advertise, e.g. in the press, on television?

You could initiate a general debate on animal rights and / or vegetarianism. Ask students to discuss the following:

- Are there any animal rights movements in your country?
- Do people feel concerned by this issue?
- Is a lot of meat consumed in your country?
- Are animals used in the cosmetic industry?

10 ENTERTAINING

WARM-UP

1 Translating

Go through the different meanings and forms of the word *entertain* in English. This word doesn't translate easily into many languages. Students can use dictionaries. Make sure everyone understands and can translate into their own language: *to entertain, entertaining, entertainment, an entertainer*. Ask students to put these words into sentences of their own.

Ask students if, when entertaining in their country, business negotiations are carried out while eating, or if people generally wait until the end of the meal as in English-speaking countries. What sort of things are eaten or drunk? Does their company spend a lot on entertaining visitors?

2 Describing

Students draw a picture either of an animal whose meat we eat or of a vegetable. They then pass it to their neighbour (Student A) who has to describe the drawing to a new partner (Student B) without saying what it is. Students A and B then decide together what vegetable or animal is being represented. They then check with the person who drew the picture.

DID YOU KNOW?

Ask students to read through the facts alone. Elicit how many different forms of entertainment are mentioned. Ask which facts concern:

– business entertainment
– food and drink
– leisure entertainment.

By this time, students should be familiar with most of the facts. Then ask them to close their books and try to remember the various dates and numbers referred to.

Finally, discuss the facts which interested them most. Ask how they would feel about being tested on their table manners! Are table manners important in their country?

LANGUAGE WORK

Pitch and intonation

1 **10.1** Students read the first part of the instructions. Play the tape once. Elicit the answer from students (a colleague / friend talking over dinner).

Ask your class to read the second part of the exercise, concerning question tags. Explain that these are often used to draw information out of people. Play the tape again.

1 Students say *Stop!* each time they hear the tags asked for in the exercise, and explain what they are referring to.

weren't you?:	B is checking that C was there last year.
didn't you?:	B is checking that C managed to get home.
has it?:	B is checking that A has been back.
am I?:	B is confirming that the story is true.

2 The speaker's voice rises in *weren't you?* and *am I?* . Explain to your class that if the tag is a real question, and the speaker expects an answer, the voice rises. If it is just asking for confirmation, the voice falls. When speaker B says ... *has it?* he is not expecting A to answer, when she throws the question back at him, he becomes less certain.

2 Students do the exercise as instructed. You may like to do this activity yourself first with a more confident student. Monitor progress, listening and checking intonation.

3 Students read the pairs of sentences and answer the questions. You may like to write the headings up on the board for students to match to the pairs of sentences.

Arguably, none of the questions would have a final rising intonation.
1, 2: suggesting
3, 4: offering
5, 6: requesting
7, 8: recommending
9, 10: asking permission

④   Students do the exercise as instructed.

a 8	c 5	e 3	g 10	i 4
b 7	d 1	f 6	h 2	j 9

You could ask students to work in pairs and read the questions and their replies to each other, paying attention to the intonation.

Being entertained

①   Students answer the questions in the quiz alone.

②   Students compare their answers with a partner. Discuss in groups:

– How far would you go to get a business contract? Where would you draw the limits?
– Is it customary to give or accept very expensive gifts when doing business in your company or country? (In the USA, for example, there are very strict laws on gift acceptance.) How do you feel about this?

Ask them how they would get out of some of the situations in the quiz.

③   Students use language for offering, suggesting, inviting, etc. to ask the questions from the quiz. Students refuse or accept.

Alternatively, you could decide if the students should refuse or accept. For example, Student A asks Student B to do karaoke. You say *Accept* to Student B who then spontaneously has to find a suitable answer to this proposition, such as: *OK, then. What's the song?*

Humour

Past simple vs past continuous vs past perfect simple

Make sure everyone knows the grammatical construction of these tenses. Review if necessary, or identify the tenses in the example sentences before doing exercise 1.

①   Students read all of the example sentences and then answer the questions.

1   past perfect simple
2   **b**: to describe someone
    h: for a long action interrupted by a short
    e: for two simultaneous continuous actions action
3   **a** and **g**: they describe past habit

②   Students do the exercise as instructed. Don't correct before playing the tape.

③   🔲10.2   First, ask your students for suggestions as to how the story ends. Play the tape while students check their answers. Ask them not to correct any mistakes while they're listening. They can put a cross next to wrong answers if they want. Ask someone to tell you the end of the story.

Play the tape again, pausing after each answer for students to check. Where students made mistakes, make sure they understand why their answer was wrong.

1	was staying	15	called
2	was	16	was wearing
3	had been	17	holding
4	wanted	18	said
5	had seen	19	said
6	said	20	walked
7	decided	21	waited
8	had read	22	waited
9	was	23	began
10	walked	24	was doing
11	tried	25	had passed
12	arrived	26	came
13	sat	27	said
14	had read		

Follow up. Discuss with students if, and how, humour should be used in various business situations, e.g. as an introduction to a presentation, during a meeting, at a business dinner.

– What are the dangers of telling jokes?
– What should you do if you don't understand a joke?
– Is humour universal?
– What kind of jokes are not acceptable?

BUSINESS SKILLS

Before beginning this section, ask students to discuss the pros and cons of business lunches and dinners, why they have them, and what they learn about a colleague or customer that they might not learn otherwise. Elicit answers concerning how they make their choice of food and drink, how they eat, their table manners, how they deal with the waiter, and how much they eat and drink.

Telling anecdotes

1 Put students into small groups. Make sure that everyone understands that an anecdote is not necessarily funny, but it is usually true, if sometimes exaggerated! For the exercise, they are inventing a story, but if students have some true experiences to draw on, the group can base their stories on those.

2 Rearrange groups so that, if possible, students are not with students from their first group. If this is not possible, two students can tell the same story, with one interrupting the other to take over. They should use expressions such as:

… and then what happened was …

… yes, but you forgot the bit about …

Make sure everyone tells their story. Pre-teach expressions such as:

Well, you know what happened to me one day …

As a follow-up, you could give students five minutes to think about a real anecdote and do the above activity again, but as a mingling exercise. Students tell their anecdote to one other person, then move on to another student and tell it again. For students who couldn't find any stories to tell, they repeat the previous student's story to the next person they mingle with.

At the restaurant

Before beginning the exercise, dictate the items below, which might be found on a menu. In groups, students put them in the order that they would expect to eat / drink them. Students can

group some of them together into courses and should decide what name to give each course.

aperitif	*fish*	*pasta salad*
bread	*ham*	*sorbet*
cake	*ice cream*	*soup*
cheese	*meat*	*whisky*
coffee	*melon*	*wine*

Focus on the photos. Students guess where the food comes from. Some students may be able to give you the names of the dishes, or at least tell you what the ingredients are.

top:	Britain
middle:	India
bottom:	Japan

1 **10.3** Students read the instructions to the exercise. Play the tape once only for students to find the answers to the first question. Use the tapescript if students are having difficulty with the names of dishes or the ingredients.

Britain:	Trout with Almonds
India:	Raita
Japan:	Sashemi

2 Students do the exercise as instructed. If your class is multinational, put students from different countries together for the improvised conversation.

3 Students do the exercise as instructed.

As a follow up, you could have a discussion about whose cuisine is the best in the world. You could begin by saying you think nothing beats British cooking, to get some reactions. See if students can come up with some reasonable parameters for their choice.

Keeping the conversation going

1 **10.4** Students read the instructions for the exercise first before listening to the tape.

> 1 They're talking about the government increasing income by raising taxation on certain things.
> 2 They have probably been talking about raising taxes generally; speaker A turns the subject to cigarettes. The conversation might move on to other unusual forms of taxation.

2 Students do the exercise as instructed. You may wish to pause after each phrase to give students time to note them down. Refer to the tapescript to check answers.

3 Class discussion. Students may be as inventive as they wish.

You could ask students how their country compares with others for income tax. Are they taxed at source, or do they make yearly declarations, etc.? Has the system of taxation changed in recent years, and if so, do students feel it has improved?

Hosting at home

1 Give students time to read through the whole passage silently. Students discuss the words in italics and any other new vocabulary. Ask your students if anyone has been invited to an Arab home and to talk about their experience. Do customs change from one Arab country to another?

palm:	the inner surface of the hand
gatherings:	meetings, usually informal
blood related:	members of the same family by birth (rather than by marriage)
customary:	usual
rug:	thick floor-mat
pampering:	treating well

2 If your class is multinational, put students from different countries together in small groups to discuss these questions. If you have Arab students in your class, try to put one, who can then initiate the questions, in each group.

Ask individual students from each group to summarize the group's comparisons.

As an extra writing activity, you could ask your students to write a passage, based on the one in their Student's Book, about hospitality in their country.

3 [10.5] Play the tape for students to listen to the conversation. When they practise reading the dialogue in pairs, they can ignore the husband's (Charlie's) part.

4 Students do the exercise as instructed. They should read through all their instructions before beginning.

If you have an equal number of male / female students, you could put your students into 'husband and wife' teams. It is often more difficult for the accompanying partner to make conversation with the host's partner as they have nothing in common to start off with. The conversation should start off with introductions, ice-breakers, offering drinks, then move on to small talk. Give students about five minutes to do this activity. This will also help prepare students for the following activity.

MEETINGS

Students read through the introduction and the aim of the meeting. Ask if any of the students have experience of this sort of campaign, so that when organizing your groups you can put one of these students in each group.

Organize students into groups. One person chairs the meeting. (Make sure that this person changes from unit to unit and encourage less confident students to take on this role.) One person takes notes. Depending on the number of students in the groups, allocate an equal number of tasks to each student. All members of the group should give their opinion, however, on each task.

If your students all live in the same town, they should use it or the nearest city.

If your class is multinational, each group will have to choose a destination for the event. Students could begin their meeting by arguing the merits of towns in their country.

Allow students time to draw up their plan of action, and ask them to present it in writing from the note-taker's notes.

One person from each group can present their group's plan of action in front of the rest of the class.

TABLE TALK

1 Focus on the photo. Students read the passage alone. Check new vocabulary and ask the two questions following the article. If you have a class of non-football lovers, you may prefer to move directly on to exercise 2.

Brainstorm other ways of increasing the number of goals scored. You could mention to students that another reason for increasing the size of the goal is that the average man is a few centimetres taller than he was when the goal size was set.

Elicit other possible changes, e.g.:

– reduce the number of players
– measure the time as in basketball
– have time out for trainers to come on
– more substitutions.

2 Class as a whole, or in small groups. This discussion may lead on to other related subjects, such as violence generally, the police, national sports in students' countries, etc.

For the last question about how students spend their leisure time, you could ask students to write, anonymously, on a piece of paper their hobbies and leisure activities and pass them to you. You read out the activities from each piece of paper, and the rest of the class has to guess who wrote them. Include your own!

3 **10.6** Students do the exercise as instructed. Play the tape once or twice, pausing after each speaker if you prefer. The first time they listen, they should try to work out which countries the speakers come from. The second time they should concentrate on the activities they mention.

1 The speaker is comparing his country, Indonesia, with Holland. Activities: in Indonesia, smoking on the streets and doing sports (men), cooking and looking after children (women); in Holland, TV, going to the pub. No difference between men and women.

2 The speaker is from Finland (this is not obvious from what she says; students may assume from her accent that she is American). She is comparing Finland and the USA (California). Activities (only women are described): in Finland, socializing with both sexes, tennis, the gym, downhill skiing, sauna; in California, shopping. House parties are common in both countries but organized differently.

3 The speaker is English and is comparing Britain with Italy, stereotyping both. Activities: in Britain, sports, gardening, DIY; in Italy, sport, especially water sports, relaxing, less organized leisure than in Britain.

11 PRESENTATIONS

WARM-UP

1 Top five fears

Brainstorm students' worst fears. Write the fears on the board and ask them to rank them, starting with the worst. Alternatively, dictate this list:

deep water
financial problems
heights
insects and bugs
speaking before a group

These are the top five worst human fears in the USA. Again, ask students to put them in order. The correct order is point 1 in the *Did You Know?* section; note that public speaking is the number one fear. Ask students what tactics they use to overcome their nerves when giving presentations.

2 Fire alarm

Ask students to imagine that they're at work when the fire alarm goes off. They have exactly five minutes to write down five items that they would take out of the building with them. Students compare their selected items. They should ask each other whether they were work-related or personal. Finally, brainstorm any difficulties students had in doing this exercise, e.g. some maybe have been stretched to find items. Ask them in what areas of their working life they are called on to prioritize things and how often they have to make snap decisions.

DID YOU KNOW?

Focus attention on the photo – where might the presentation be taking place? Do students ever give such high-tech presentations?

Give students time to read the section silently. Get feedback on what they consider to be the most important or useful piece of information. Then ask who has given presentations. Find out the following:

– When was it?
– What was it about?
– How did it go?

– What skills did you feel you lacked?
– How nervous did you feel?

Ask students about presentations they have attended. What made them good or bad?

Do not spend too much time on this at this stage; students will analyse their presentation skills later in the unit.

LANGUAGE WORK

Sentence stress

1 Students read through the instructions and text. Find the stressed words in the first sentence with them, to make sure everyone understands how to proceed: *First, coming, Marketing*. Students work in pairs and read the text to each other.

> Answers are in bold in the tapescript on page 184 in the Student's Book.

2 **11.1** Play the tape once. Students compare with their own indications of word stress. Discuss differences which surprised them. Some of their versions, if different, could be perfectly feasible, so correction to this exercise should be flexible.

3 Students complete the exercise alone. Correct together.

> 1 F
> 2 F
> 3 T (**don't** follow, **not** know)
> 4 T (**current** scenario, **present** situation, **last** year)

4 Students do the exercise as instructed. You may wish to play the tape again for choral or individual repetition.

Whatever turns you on
Phrasal / prepositional verbs

First, students should read through the example sentences. Check that students understand the meanings of the verbs. They should use dictionaries for this exercise. If you speak your students' language, you may have to translate. Check they understand the title of the section, again using dictionaries.

You could ask students to make other sentences using all of these phrasal verbs, to check they can use them in the right context.

1   Students answer questions 1 and 2 as instructed.

1 b, d, e	2 a, c, f, g

This area of grammar can be difficult even for advanced students. Reference books often use the term *phrasal verb* to mean any verb made up of two or more words; they behave differently according to whether the particle is an adverb or a preposition, and whether the verb is transitive or intransitive. If your class is advanced enough, you may wish to present the other two types of phrasal verb: those that take no object, e.g. *The plane took off* vs *He took off his hat*; and those where the object must be between the verb and the preposition / adverb particle, e.g. *Let me take you through the main parts*.

Summarize the four types of phrasal / prepositional verbs and go through page 164 in the Reference section with students.

You may want to take a few simple verbs such as *make*, *do*, *look*, *go*, *come*, *take*, etc. and brainstorm the phrasal verbs students already know, then ask them to put them into sentences. Don't add any more. Students will be surprised to see how many they are already familiar with. You may also cover some of the phrasal verbs in the following exercise.

2   Give students some examples of how the exercise should be done, e.g.:
*We will **examine** their proposal before lunch.*
*We will **go over** it before lunch.*

Students can use dictionaries to help them if they wish.

1	set aside	6	take over
2	put off	7	think over
3	set up	8	look at
4	carry out	9	fill in / out
5	run through	10	put down

In sentence 1, the preposition changes *(set aside $1.5 bn for)*.

3   Again, give an example of how this exercise should be done. Define the noun *a takeover*: the acquisition of a company by another, generally a larger one. Some of the words can be used as nouns or verbs; you may wish to make the exercise simpler by specifying which form they should use (note that *turnkey* is an adjective). Students work in pairs and check their definitions together. You could extend the exercise by asking for example sentences for each word.

Some of these words can be used as nouns or verbs; they are all defined here as nouns unless otherwise stated.

A	
cutback:	reduction in resources allocated for something (e.g. in production, personnel)
outlook:	expectation / prospect for future
sellout:	event for which all tickets have been sold
trade-in:	something given in part exchange for something else; staff replacement
turnover:	the total business done by an organization in a given period
upgrade:	increase in importance or value
upturn:	upward turn, trend, curve
write-off:	cancelled from accounts, abandoned as worthless

B	
intake:	taking in of food, staff, air etc.
layout:	plan or arrangement (e.g. of pages, offices)
mark-up:	amount of increase in price, often expressed as a percentage
offset:	something that balances, counteracts or compensates for something else
output:	work / amount produced by person / machine; result from processing
outlet:	agency / market / retail store
trade-off:	compromise
turnkey(adj):	built and handed over ready for use (i.e. constructor / installer is responsible from design to completion)

BUSINESS SKILLS

Preparing the presentation

1 Students answer the question alone, then compare in groups. Discuss together and elicit other tasks.

2 Put students into groups of three or four to discuss the questions. One person should make short written summaries of the group's answers.

3 **11.2** Play the tape once or twice for students to match the extracts with the questions. Compare and correct together.

1	b	3	e	5	d
2	c	4	a	6	f

Use the tapescript to compare students' answers for exercise 2 with the speakers' answers. Students could comment on how useful the advice given is.

Audience attention

1 Before doing the exercise, ask students to plot a curve indicating how their attention fluctuates during one of your lessons. Ask them if they think the same curve could represent their attention during a presentation.

Discuss questions 1–3 together: The most important points of a presentation must be made at the beginning and end. During the middle part of the presentation when attention is low, all kinds of variations or devices are needed – various visual aids, demonstrations, questions, hints at what is coming next, a coffee break, etc. Attention will only rise at the end if the audience know they're near the end, so route mapping is critical.

2 Students do the exercise as instructed. Ideas can include visual aids, questionnaires for participants to fill in, asking questions.

Speaking from notes

1 Students read through the whole exercise and look at the prompt card in the Student's Book. Check that they understand the abbreviations:

(V)SB	:	(Very) Small Business
IT	:	Information Technology
B	:	Billion
M	:	Million
T	:	Thousand

Before students begin discussing the three questions asked, you may want to review linking words and phrases used to introduce various parts of a presentation. See the Reference section on pages 166–167 of the Student's Book.

You could put your students into small groups and ask each member to prepare one part of the presentation.

2 **11.3** Students should read the instructions and questions before you play the tape. Discuss the answers to the questions together.

Answers to this section will be subjective, and others are possible. The following are suggested answers:

1 he takes into account that the audience is large and knowledgeable about the subject, so his speech is measured but not too slow
2 by using extreme words like *thrilled*, *excited*, *incredible*, etc., by praising the audience and their product, by giving a lot of impressive statistics
3 by using sequence markers (see tapescript)
4 yes

Remind students that much of the impact and success of a presentation depends not just on your voice, but on your facial expression and other body language. If you have access to video with your students, you could incorporate some videos into your lessons to show this.

You could ask students to compare the delivery of the speaker in 11.1 with this presentation.

Using visual aids

1 Students should look back at the prompt card and discuss the answers to the questions with a partner or in groups. (Note that *slide* refers to any kind of overhead projections or graphics used in software programs.)

The bar chart is useful for comparing two or more sets of figures for any given year. It is not as useful for presenting precise figures, or two sets of contrasting figures if the difference is slight.

The line graph is more suitable for showing the progression of a set of figures over a period of time. It is also useful to show two or more contrasting sets of figures, especially if the lines cross over each other.

The table gives precise data, but does not show the information in a visually stimulating way, or emphasize any of the figures.

The main image is the most successful presentation of this set of figures; it is eye-catching and emphasizes the most important information, which is that sales are continuing to rise and have passed $1m.

The statement *In 5 years sales are up 115%* is perhaps even more striking and direct than the main image. However, it ignores the stages in which the increase was achieved.

2 Ask students to discuss in pairs, then take feedback as a whole class.

MEETINGS

Students read through the whole section alone. Ask if anyone can give you a definition of *e-business* (also known as *e-commerce*): using the Internet to buy and sell products and services. There is a presentation framework on pages 166–167 of the Reference section in the Student's Book. You could use this to revise presentation language and skills, or students could use it as a checklist as they prepare their presentation. Alternatively, you could use it as the basis for a separate discussion; students who frequently give presentations may have differing views on how to go about it. On page 168 there are some factors for judging someone's performance when delivering a presentation.

If your students never do e-business, you may prefer to use one of the alternative presentations suggested below. Students can either work alone or in small groups for these:

– a presentation that students really will have to do in the near future (whether it is in their own language or in English)
– certain aspects of their department or company
– their country / town
– topical issues which concern their companies
– any other subject of students' choice.

Any of these could also be used as a writing activity. Ask students to prepare a written report on one of the above subjects.

TABLE TALK

1 Brainstorm the sort of subjects the two women may or may not talk about: brothers, sisters, parents, children, husbands, etc. Write these up on the board to compare after listening to the tape.

1 [11.4] Play the tape twice if necessary. Note that the Japanese woman is an actress, hence the reference to her father's costume business and following in his footsteps.

> Students' answers will vary. The important points are:
>
> Speaker A comes from India, where her parents still live. Her father had his own business and her mother was a teacher of English and Italian; now they are both retired. She has a sister living in Germany.
>
> Speaker B is an only child, an actress, and comes from Japan. Her mother lives in Tokyo and in common with others of her generation did not go out to work. Her father, who died ten years ago, was a costume maker.

2 Ask students to repeat phrases and questions they heard that showed interest, e.g.:

Oh, how interesting. Is that unusual?

Check in the tapescript on page 184 of the Student's Book for the expressions they use.

3 Students work with a partner. You could ask pairs to volunteer to carry out their conversation in front of the rest of the class.

2 Class discussion, or in small groups if your class is big. Ask students if they can think of other sources of stress not mentioned in the table.

Continue with the rest of the exercise as instructed.

You could follow up exercise 2 by discussing different ways of dealing with stress and how effective students think they are. Try to avoid students going into detail about their personal situations! You could take some of the less personal situations mentioned in both parts of exercise 2 and find ways of dealing with them.

12 PERFORMANCE

WARM-UP

1 Physical performance

Ask students to stand in pairs against the walls of the classroom. Ask them to stretch, in turns, as high as they can up the wall with their fingers outstretched. The student who is not stretching makes a light pencil mark on the wall to mark where their partner has reached. Then ask them to repeat the procedure and really stretch themselves.

Get feedback on how much better they performed the second time round – most will average about 5–10% (though some might actually perform worse). Ask students what they have learned from this exercise. Why do we hold some percentage of our talent in reserve? What difference would it make to their companies if they (or the company as a whole) performed 10% better?

2 Performance-related pay

Ask students to imagine that salaries were fixed on the basis of someone's performance. For example, a teacher would be paid more in proportion to how many of his / her students passed their exams, and with what grades. Students analyse how some of the following professions could be given performance-related salaries and what the consequences of such a system would be: doctor, lawyer, accountant, prime minister, priest, cook, and any others you or they decide.

DID YOU KNOW?

Before students read this section, ask them to say what percentage quality they should be aiming at in their products or services: 90%, 95%, 99%, or 99.9%. Then tell them to open their Student's Book and read the first fact in the *Did You Know?* section, which shows the consequences of accepting 99.9% quality.

Students work in pairs. Student A reads facts 1, 3, 5, 7, 9, and 10 while Student B reads facts 2, 4, 6, 8, 10. Students prepare one question about each of their five facts. Then students read their partner's

facts. Students ask each other their questions without looking at the book.

Discuss which facts interested or surprised them most.

The photo shows the New York Marathon. You may wish to discuss with students other measures of personal success, particularly if they themselves participate in them.

LANGUAGE WORK

Intonation in praise and criticism

1 Students do the exercise as instructed. Correct after students have listened to the tape.

2 [12.1] Play the tape while students check if their choices for exercise 1 are correct. Play the tape again, stopping after each sentence for correction. You may wish to ask students to repeat the sentences after the speakers, to practise intonation.

1	P	4	C	7	P
2	C	5	P	8	C
3	C	6	C	9	P / C

Students then complete the sentences as instructed and practise reading them with a partner.

3 [12.2] Ask students to listen for the reasons for the manager's praise or criticism. Play the tape once for students to identify whether praise or criticism is being offered in each case, and a second time for students to complete the table with the reason.

Item	Praise	Criticism
engine	it's going to out-perform competitors	
gas consumption	it should go down by 5%	
ignition	the way he's resolved the problem	

Item	Praise	Criticism
budget		it's way over the allocated amount
schedule		the project is behind schedule

4   Play the tape again. Ask students to say *Stop!* when they hear an expression used to praise or criticize.

Discuss the question about why she begins by praising his work. This is because it's generally better to begin on a positive note and get the person on your side before you start criticizing them.

Discuss the remaining questions. Ask students how often they are praised by their boss and whether this is less or more than the criticism they receive.

Finally, ask them to read the tapescript aloud, practising the intonation.

For further practice, you could ask your students to note down two or three achievements in their life. Working in pairs, they take turns to recount their achievements while their partner praises them. You could do this first yourself with a more confident student.

5   Ask students to work with a new partner. Students should read through the whole of their instructions on pages 138 and 145 before beginning the role-play. When they have finished, you could ask pairs to volunteer to do their role-play in front of the rest of the class.

Ability and permission

allow, can, enable, let, permit

Modal verbs are an area of difficulty even at this level. This section and the next look at functional language appropriate to the theme of this unit, where modal verbs are commonly used. Other functional areas are covered in the Reference section. For a comprehensive list of modal verbs and their structure, refer students to a grammar reference book.

1   Students can discuss the answers to the questions in pairs. Correct together.

> *Allow, enable, permit* take the infinitive (with *to*)
> *Let* and *can* take the bare infinitive (without *to*)
> 1   a   This program lets you add things …
>   b   This command lets you edit …
>   c   This software lets you dictate letters by voice …
>   d   Tool Y lets you import and export data.
> 2   a   You can add things manually with this program …
>   b   You can edit documents with this command, and you can do graphics with this one.
>   c   You can dictate letters by voice …
>   d   You can import and export data with Tool Y.

Go through page 160 in the Reference section.

2   Students can work alone, or in pairs if they are from the same country or company. Elicit some examples before they begin. Ask if they are allowed to smoke in their office, if they can choose their working hours, etc.

Continue as instructed.

Finally, ask one pair to volunteer to read their lists in front of the rest of the class. Make sure that all forms of *allowed / not allowed* have been used; if not, summarize the following with your class:

We're allowed to …
We can …
They let us …
… is allowed

Go over the negative and interrogative forms of these.

Students from some countries tend to use *it is possible to* instead of these verbs. Point out that while this is correct, they should try to use the other forms too.

3   Class discussion. Encourage students to use the forms they have just practised.

As a follow up, you could ask students to discuss the advances of other products or sectors, e.g. photography, household appliances, or cars.

Describing performance

Students can discuss the answers to exercises 1–3 in small groups or class as a whole. Exercise 4 is a writing activity; you could set this as homework if appropriate.

> 1   an advertisement: *essential, fully integrated, revolutionary, prompt, best-in-class technologies* are some of the extreme terms typical of advertisements
>
>   You could also draw attention to repetition of the product name, presenting the product as the answer to all the reader's problems, and use of (advertising space is expensive).
>
> 2   informal and quite simple: addressing the reader as *you*, use of abbreviations, incomplete sentences (*All of which lets you…*), use of imperatives

Obligations
have to, must, should

● Let students read though all the example sentences first. Students should answer the questions alone then compare with a partner. Correct together.

> 1   *Helmets must be worn* … in **b**
> 2   *don't have to* in **c**
>   in **d**, something is forbidden
> 3   *should* in **f**
>   *must* in **e** indicates obligation
> 4   **g**; *should really have* in **h**
> 5   **j** (the speaker may or may not have gone in **i**, we are only told that it wasn't necessary)
>   *didn't have to* in **i**
> 6   **i**: because it was cancelled.
>   **j**: because it was a waste of time.

Go through page 160 in the Reference section if your students need more work on these forms.

● Students work alone. Correct together.

> 1   have to   4   didn't have to do
> 2   should have told   5   should
> 3   mustn't, must

● Students discuss the questions with a partner or in small groups. At the end of the activity, share some of the answers. Monitor progress, listening in to make sure that students are making the correct distinction between *must*, *have to* and *should*, etc.

BUSINESS SKILLS
Company performance

● The photos show British Airways tailplanes as they have developed over the years according to the company's changing corporate image. The order is: 1, 5, 3, 4, 2.

Students discuss questions 1–3 in groups. Ask them to talk about their own company and to compare it with their competitors. Ask them to try and think of examples of companies whose performance is influenced by their perceived image.

Tell them to think of major companies in their country and describe the public image of these. Are they seen as being old-fashioned, trendy, caring, unscrupulous, reliable, etc.?

● Students can work with a partner to rank the factors, and to discuss the questions that follow. Other important factors might be:
- leadership
- autonomy
- control
- people involvement
- market orientation
- innovation
- integrity (of people and of the product).

Financial statements

① **12.3** Play the tape once or twice. Ask students to make notes while they are listening and then to answer the questions. Correct together.

> 1   yes, it was a record performance
> 2   40%
> 3   the strength of the dollar
> 4   twenty years
> 5   the same thing
> 6   the Far East and the Pacific Basin
> 7   the media sector

② Students work alone, using dictionaries if necessary. Correct together. Many of the terms in this exercise are open to interpretation. The answers given are for British financial statements. Even within the same country, accountants may classify them in different ways. Students may therefore disagree with some of the definitions and also about where they may appear.

> 1   d   3   b   5   c   7   i   9   g
> 2   a   4   e   6   f   8   j   10 h

③ Students do the exercise as instructed.

> The first definition is of a Profit and Loss Account
> (also called a *Trading Account*), the second
> definition is of a Balance Sheet.
> Balance sheet: 1, 2, 4
> Profit and Loss Account: 3, 5, 6, 7, 8
> 9: invoices, price list
> 10: annual accounts statement

④ As instructed, students choose one of the topics and work alone to prepare their presentation, which should last no more than five minutes. Less confident students may prefer to work in pairs.

Elicit some of the key words needed to make the speech more effective, e.g. *record performance, landmark year, significant milestone.*

Personal and group performance

① Put students into small groups. Give them time to read through all the tasks, alone, before answering the question.

Students estimate the time they would take to perform the tasks. They compare with the rest of the group.

② Ask students to carry out the three shortest tasks and to compare how long they thought they would take with the time they actually took. What do they conclude from this?

Correct using the key on page 152 of the Student's Book. For some questions, other answers are possible. Answers are not provided for numbers 2 and 7.

MEETINGS

Give students time to read through the whole section. Divide the class into groups of five or six. They can allocate roles among themselves; members of the board should include directors from all the major departments in a company. Allocate one person to chair the meeting and another to take notes.

At the end of the activity, students could prepare a written plan of action.

As an alternative meeting, and making use of the factors listed for performance criteria, give students these instructions:

–   The head of your department is retiring. Your company has a policy of promoting from within if possible. Your task is to choose the best person for the job.
–   Rank the performance criteria factors in order of importance. Then each student should write a brief fictitious resume of a suitable candidate for the job. Each person in the group then reads the resumes of each candidate. Who is the best possible contender? No student can recommend his / her own candidate.

TABLE TALK

1 Students work in groups. If they have difficulty thinking of more factors, you could suggest some or all of the following:

- amount given to poor countries in aid
- birth and death rates
- crime
- national debt
- investment in education
- environmental record
- exchange / inflation rates
- industrial and agricultural output
- inventiveness (number of patents registered)
- sport
- tax system
- transport system
- unemployment rate
- visible and invisible trade

2 Students work alone and compare with a partner. You could write up the list on the board and do a survey to find out which factor came up most or least often, and ask students to explain and justify their answers.

3 **12.4** Play the tape once for students to tick the points mentioned in the list in exercise 2. Ask students to read through the rest of the questions before playing the tape again. Answers can be discussed with the class as a whole, or in small groups.

The speakers came from the UK and Australia (conversation 1), Germany and New Zealand (2), and Germany and Italy (3).

conversation 1:	personal appearance, money, intelligence, class
conversation 2:	money, class, position in society, house, education, career position, amount of free time
conversation 3:	career, money, house and car, success of children

13 NEGOTIATING

WARM-UP

1 Negotiating topics

Brainstorm which of the following negotiations students would have most difficulty with:

- negotiating a pay rise with their boss
- negotiating / bargaining at an open air market in a foreign country, where they don't speak the language
- negotiating pocket money with your child
- negotiating a marriage contract with their future husband / wife.

2 Name your price

Write up the English expression *Every man has his price* on the board. Ask students to tell you what they understand by this expression. Then ask students to list three things that they would never do, even if someone paid them vast quantities of money. These could include particular jobs, places they would never live in, relationships they wouldn't get involved in, moral issues, etc. In groups of three or four, students combine their lists and try and choose the worst two and the best two. They then try to establish just how much money it would take for them to do the activities in question, and whether everyone really does have a price or not.

DID YOU KNOW?

Ask students to read through the whole section. They then decide which two quotations represent the best pieces of negotiation advice for them, and explain why. Ask them if there are any pieces of advice they don't agree with and why. Do they apply these pieces of advice when negotiating?

The photo shows the statue of Justice on the Old Bailey Law Courts in London.

LANGUAGE WORK

Pronunciation and spelling

Focus on the image of the word tree. If your students come from countries where these languages are spoken, ask them to continue giving you other forms of the word *negotiate*. If they speak other languages, ask them if they know the derivation of the word.

1 Allow students time to read through the whole passage. Discuss the text together, and ask students to explain where they have difficulty with English spelling.

2 Examples of the unpredictable three per cent include:

- numbers: *one, two, four, eight, once*
- modals and auxiliaries: *could, would, do, does, are, was, were, has, have*, etc.

3
1 Students work alone. Do not correct until students have listened to the tape.
2 13.1 Play the tape. Students compare their answers. Correct together.

action	discussion
complexion	sugar
conscious	
Other words:	
chance: /ʧ/	scheme: /s/
edge: /ʤ/	science: /s/
pleasure: /ʒ/	vision: /ʒ/
scene: /s/	

Negotiating styles

1 13.2 Students read through the whole exercise before listening to the tape. Correct together, using the tapescript at the back of the Student's Book, if necessary, to look for exact definitions of the words.

1 getting something below its price
2 talking things over, not necessarily reaching a conclusion
3 finding out about home and family as well
4 mutual discussion, the best for both parties

2 Students do the matching exercise as instructed. These idioms are used in 13.3 , and this exercise will familiarize students with some of the expressions which are used either during negotiations or when talking about them. Explain to students that while they should be able to recognize and understand these expressions, they shouldn't try to use them all.

1 b	3 e	5 g	7 i	9 h
2 a	4 f	6 c	8 d	10 j

3 There are no correct answers to exercise 1. Students rate the qualities and compare their answers with a partner or in groups.

2 13.3 Play the tape for students to circle the qualities and compare with their ratings.

All qualities except sense of humour are mentioned.

3 Play the tape again. Ask students to say *Stop!* when they hear the expressions from exercise 2.

All the expressions are mentioned.

Go through the tapescript at the back of the book for students to underline or highlight these expressions. You could ask them to replace the expressions with the definitions given in exercise 2. You could also ask them to find equivalent expressions in their own language.

When students have completed the listening task get some feedback about the consultant's views on honesty.

– What did he say you should be honest about? (price, terms of contract)
– What two ploys does he mention? (implying he has a better offer to consider, suggesting

they have reached stalemate and need a break)
– What is the point of the second ploy? (making the other party wait)

Concessions

First and second conditional

Ask students to read all the example sentences.

1 Students should work alone, then compare their answers with a partner. Correct together.

1 *would*
2 first conditional
3 *Unless you* can only be used in sentence **e**
4 *if* can replace *whether* only in sentence **h**
5 yes
6 no

For further explanation, see page 155 in the Reference section.

2 Students do the exercise as instructed.

1 If, 's
2 on the condition, can
3 reduced, would
4 Provided that, will clinch
5 Although …

3 Put your class into groups. First, you could brainstorm the sort of situations that are negotiated between the groups of people in the exercise, e.g.:
– child / parent: pocket money, staying out late
– wife / husband: holidays, housekeeping budget.

At the end of the activity, ask students to discuss elements that are common to business and non-business negotiations.

4 Students work in pairs. Monitor progress to make sure the expressions from exercise 2 are being used. You could extend the exercise with other situations, such as supplier / customer, employer / employee, buyer / seller, etc.

BUSINESS SKILLS

Pre-negotiation socializing

This business skills section is designed to take students through the various stages of a negotiation, from the pre-negotiation and initial contact stage to the follow-up letters before the contract is finally signed.

1 Students should read through the passage alone. Then discuss the three different cultures and compare with students' own countries. Tell them about business culture in your country. Ask them if they are used to doing business with other countries, and to tell you about business culture there. Which way of doing business do they prefer?

2 When students have finished discussing these points among themselves, you could ask them to give each others' opinions, using the third person, in front of the rest of the group and say if they agree or disagree. You may wish to go through phrases to contrast two points of view, such as:

on the one hand
on the other hand
whereas
however

You could extend this section with a role-play. Students work in pairs. Student A is interested in doing business with Student B's company. A doesn't know B personally, but has been given B's phone number via a third party. A phones B to arrange a pre-negotiation socializing event, which students decide themselves. Students role-play the phone call and the event.

At the table

1 Write each group's suggestions on the board. Elicit the following if students don't suggest them:

- price
- terms of payment
- delivery
- installation
- training
- advertising
- consultancy
- maintenance
- warranty
- reliability
- import / export duties

Students put them in order of difficulty and discuss their lists with a partner. Finish with a class discussion to find out which items were generally considered the most or least difficult.

2 Students read through the phrases and answer the question as instructed.

1–2 **13.4** Students discuss the phrases; don't correct at this stage. Play the tape once for students to check their answers. The extracts are not in the same order as they appear on the tape. Ask students to say *Stop!* when they hear the phrases.

a B	d S	g S	i B
b B,E	e B	h B,E	j B
c B,E	f S		

3 Students read through the whole exercise and write their answers next to the questions. They can do this with a partner if they prefer, or compare answers once they have finished.

Play the tape again to listen for the answers. Correct together.

1 a, f, e, b, d, c
2 price, licence agreement
3 hardware costs have increased, investment in a new system
4 $4,900
5 no

You could ask students to work in pairs and read the dialogue from the tapescript at the back of the Student's Book. They should highlight or underline the phrases they feel they will be able to use in their own negotiations.

Presenting your case

This is an exercise on business ethics; you may need to exercise care if any of your students work for companies whose practices match any of those in the list.

Students read through the list in exercise 1.

1 Students work alone to choose the two companies.

② Students do the exercise as instructed. You could ask groups to volunteer to do their negotiation in front of the rest of the class. If you wish to make the exercise more formal, you could ask students to prepare a presentation of their case for the two companies they have chosen; see Unit 11 and pages 166–168 in the Reference section in the Student's Book.

The negotiation game

Discuss the quotation; do students agree? An extract from Karrass's book *Negotiate to Close* appears on page 62 of the Workbook.

Students work in pairs. First, they should read through the whole section. Start by discussing the notion of company perks. Are perks a more effective way of motivating people than higher salaries? Which perks do they have in their jobs? Can they think of any others that they would rather have?

① Discuss with the whole class first what kind of perks are likely to appeal to Student A and Student B; students then decide which role they are going to play.

② Once they have identified their four items, students rank them in order of importance, starting with the most important.

③ Students proceed as instructed. You could extend the exercise by brainstorming any further perks they feel Students A and B would appreciate.

MEETINGS

Meeting to negotiate

Allocate Student A and B roles. Allow students time to read through their role and their terms of negotiation; Student B's information is on page 145 of the Student's Book. Students should be aware of each other's role, but Student B should not read Student A's target terms.

Before beginning the negotiation, students could look again at the tapescript for ⬛13.4 and the expressions introduced in exercise 2 in the *Negotiating styles* section. Let your students make

notes first before beginning the meeting, if they prefer.

Monitor progress and give help where necessary. You may wish to ask pairs to role-play their negotiation in front of the rest of the class after the activity is finished.

Afterwards, ask for feedback about what students found the most difficult or the easiest perk to negotiate with their partner.

As a writing activity, you could ask students to write a letter confirming all the terms agreed upon during the negotiation.

TABLE TALK

① Students focus on the photos and the title of the text. Before reading the text, ask them what they think it will be about.

Students then read the text, which is an extract from an article summarizing Ralph Rene's book. Ask a few questions to check comprehension.

② ⬛13.5 Give students time to read through the questions. It would be useful if you could bring in a camera and a few photos (in and out of focus) to explain some of the vocabulary needed for the listening exercise.

Play the tape once straight through. Students can discuss with a partner the answers they heard.

Play the tape again for students to find the rest of the answers, pausing at the appropriate places. Make sure different students answer. If they didn't understand, play that part of the tape again.

1	1961, because America was behind in the space race
2	no, they filmed from a TV screen in Houston
3	no
4	they wore fat pressurized gloves
5	2 metres

③ Class discussion. Ask students whether they think more or less money should be spent on space research.

14 TRADE

In this final unit there is no grammar section, and no new functional language is taught. Instead, in the context of domestic and international trade, students have the opportunity to review most of the language from the other thirteen units.

WARM-UP

1 World trade

Ask students to imagine this situation: At 12.00 tomorrow, world trade will cease. In groups, ask students to imagine the consequences. This should involve them talking about the purposes of international trade. Ask students to consider beyond the economic reasons and to consider issues such as:

- increasing variety of goods and services available
- improving standards of living
- getting countries to communicate better with each other and to be more dependent on each other.

2 Economic freedom

Ask students to discuss how much economic freedom there is in their country, i.e. how far government intervention affects economic relations. To focus their discussion, elicit the following economic indicators:

- trade policy
- taxation
- monetary policy
- the banking system
- foreign investment rules
- property rights
- the amount of economic output consumed by the government
- regulation policy
- the size of the black market
- the extent of wage and price controls.

DID YOU KNOW?

Focus on the photo. Ask students if they know what it represents (Crystal Palace exhibition of 1851).

Students then read all the facts in the *Did You Know?* section. Ask them to find all the collocations with the word *trade* in the section: *trade fair, trademark, trade union, trade secret*. Ask them if they can think of others: *trade department, trade agreement, dispute, name, press*, etc.

Ask students to compare some of the facts with the situation in their own country, e.g.:

- How are unions organized in their country (e.g. by trade as in Britain, by political association as in France)?
- How does patenting work?
- Are trade fairs common?

LANGUAGE WORK

Pronunciation and stress

Before students open their books, ask them if there are any British and American place names they have particular difficulty in pronouncing. Make a list on the board and ask students to practise saying them.

1 [14.1] Read the example to students and give the answer to make sure they understand what to do: *Austin* rhymes with *loss*.

They then complete the exercise, as instructed.

1	item	5	method	8	done
2	ship	6	few	9	thorough
3	enough	7	best	10	pressure
4	when				

2 Again, read the example to your class.

Students complete the exercise and compare with a partner. Correct together.

1	Wisconsin	4	Geneva
2	Madrid	5	Michigan
3	Cuba		

Note that British and American pronunciation differs fairly systematically with regard to names of people and places, e.g. *Birmingham*, where *ham* in the USA is pronounced like *ham* in *hamburger*. As a general rule British place names have the stress on the first syllable, as do people's surnames and first names.

Trade fairs

Students do the exercise as instructed. They should use dictionaries, if available, to check the words in italics. Students can discuss questions 1 and 2 in pairs or small groups.

shrinks:	gets smaller (i.e. quicker to travel around)
trade fairs:	exhibition of goods from the same area of industry or commerce
boomed:	become more successful
plenty of headaches:	worry
target customers:	potential clients whose business you wish to attract
investment / return ratio:	how much you gain in proportion to the cost involved
weighed up:	considered
breaking into:	entering (with difficulty)
checking out:	investigating
suppliers:	providers of the raw materials a business needs to produce its goods
distributors:	agents or representatives who sell your goods in a given area
retailers:	those who sell directly to the public
shop around:	compare prices and services from one supplier to another
direct consumer input:	feedback and opinions that come directly from the end users of the product

forums:	meeting place
seminars:	study groups for small numbers of delegates
attendees:	those participating in a meeting
customs authorities:	government department that collects taxes on imported goods
infrastructure:	the different parts that together make up a whole system; here, the services provided by the parties mentioned in the paragraph

Do business, make money

1 14.2 Students do the exercise as instructed.

2	V	5	V	8	V
3	E	6	E or V	9	E
4	E	7	V	10	E

When students have completed the task, play each sentence individually and elicit the sentences and questions. These, along with those in exercise 2, will be helpful for the role-play in exercise 3.

2 This exercise is an opportunity to review modal and auxiliary verbs; see pages 154 and 160–161 in the Reference section if students need further help.

1 Students do the exercise as instructed. Don't correct before playing the tape.

2 14.3 Play the tape, stopping after each answer to correct exercise 1.

3 Play the tape again. Ask students to note where any additional words or phrases are without actually writing them down. Then play the tape again, pausing after each addition, and elicit what was said.

The additional words and phrases are:
actually, well, that'd be great, I mean, ah, (It is omitted), well I have to say, certainly, yes, why not?, right, I'll look forward to that

Discuss the purpose of these discourse markers (to make the conversation flow, and sound more natural).

3 Role-play. In pairs, students read the instructions, and choose roles. You may wish your class to do the role-play a second time, changing partners and roles.

Making contact

1 Students should first read through the whole section.

1 First, students put the verbs in the dialogue into the correct tenses (this revises many of the tenses that they have come across in the book). They should do this part of the exercise individually.

2 Working in pairs, students write the visitor's side of the conversation. Correct together. Answers suggested below are for both parts of the exercise.

Suggested answers (other answers are possible):

a ... I'm so pleased you rang.

b How are you?

   I'm ... Did you have ...

c I just wondered if you had prepared the quotation I asked you for.

   ... I haven't had ... We have been ... we got ... we didn't expect ...

d Well, can I ask you a couple of questions?

   ... would you like ...

e How soon can I expect delivery?

   You can expect ...

f How long is the warranty?

   It would be covered ... nothing ever goes wrong.

g How often should it be serviced?

   It should be serviced ...

h Where would / are repairs (be) carried out?

   ... repairs would be / are carried out ...

i How do I contact you if there's an urgent problem?

   We have ... you don't have to worry ...

j Thank you for the information.

   ... I'll get / I can get ...

---

2 Role-play. You may wish to revise the section on reported speech on page 169 in the Reference section first. You could also go over phrases used to ask what other people said:

And what did he say about ...?
Did you ask him about ...?
He told me ...

BUSINESS SKILLS

Trading terms

Students should read through the whole activity before writing in the answers. Let students use dictionaries or ask each other for the meaning of words they don't know.

Use the key on page 153 of the Student's Book for correction.

You could use questions 4 and 5 for the basis of a discussion on free trade associations. Some other FTAs or similar are: The West African Economic and Monetary Union (WAEMU), The League of Arab States, Latin American Economic System (SELKA), OPEC.

Problems

1 Students work alone to match the complaints and responses. They can check with a partner. Correct together.

1	d	4	c	6	g
2	b	5	f	7	e
3	a				

c is an apology; the others are explanations or excuses

As a follow up, you could ask students to discuss in what areas of life they have to complain (e.g. restaurants, services, shops), and how they feel when they have to do this. How do they react when they are on the receiving end of complaints? Do they apologize, defend themselves, play for time, get confused?

2 **14.4** Play the tape, pausing after each extract to allow students to write their answers.

1   late payment
2   late delivery
3   faulty system
4   maintenance not available
5   wrong quantity
6   cancelled order
7   bad translation
8   performance not in line with specifications

Students should use phrases from the responses in the previous exercise to reply to these complaints. Play the tape once again, pausing after each extract, and asking individual students to respond to the speakers on the tape.

3   Students choose one or two of the situations from exercises 1 and 2 and perform a telephone role-play. If necessary review telephone language from Unit 1 before starting. If you do not have access to telephones, you may prefer to conduct the role-play as a meeting.

As a follow up writing activity, you could ask students to write to their partner, apologizing for the error, confirming what they plan to do to correct it, and possibly offering some sort of compensation to the customer.

MEETINGS

If you haven't done the *Meetings* section on e-business in Unit 11, introduce this exercise with a discussion about the Internet. Discuss the following:

– How much time do you or your company spend on it?
– What do you use it for?
– What do you like most / least about it?
– Should it be controlled, or access restricted?
– What do you imagine its future to be?

Students then read through steps 1–3.

Organize your class into groups of four or five and let them allocate roles among themselves. How technical the discussion becomes will depend on students' background and skills. If students do not have access to the Internet, you may prefer to conduct this exercise as setting up a terrestrial

trade fair; most of the tasks can be carried out without adaptation.

One person should chair the discussion while another takes notes.

TABLE TALK

1   Students read through the extracts on their own and then do the discussion part of the activity in small groups.

2   **14.5** Play the tape for students to make notes on how the extracts continue. They write a brief summary and compare it with a partner's.

Answers will vary, but the following is a brief summary of each system.

Silent trade is a barter system that avoids the need to meet face to face. The first group leave some goods in a clearing and withdraw from view. The second group come out of hiding, inspect the goods, and leave goods of their own which they consider to be of equivalent value. The first group inspect the second set of goods and if they are satisfied they take them and leave their own. Otherwise they leave the goods and the second group decide whether to leave more or retrieve their own. The process is repeated until both sides are satisfied with the goods they are to receive.

Bartercard began 1990s in Australia. It allows people to advertise their services, which are valued by Bartercard and offered for barter. The public use the service they need, and then pay for it at a later date by providing their own service to the same value.

3   Students do the exercise as instructed. Ask groups who devise a new bartering system to present this to the rest of the class.

4   Students play the game as instructed on page 153 of the Student's Book. You may wish to review the instructions yourself before playing the game!

ACTIVITY 1

Two-minute test in communication

① Read all the instructions before you start. Do not speak to anyone.

② Write today's date in the top left hand corner of this page.

③ Delete the word *date* in sentence two.

④ Draw four small circles in the bottom right hand corner of this page.

⑤ Underline the word *communication* in the title of this test.

⑥ Put a cross next to all the even numbers in this test.

⑦ Draw a circle around number 5.

⑧ Write your surname in the space after this question.

....

⑨ If you think you have successfully completed the instructions so far raise your right hand, if you're not sure go back to sentence two and check all your answers carefully.

⑩ If you are satisfied with your answers, stand up.

⑪ Now that you have completed the test as instructed in sentence 1, carry out only sentence eight.

ACTIVITY 2

Product duration

Estimate what the duration of each product below is in years (for example, a fridge typically lasts 15 years before having to be replaced). Then do the same for the duration of rubbish.

Discuss and justify your answers with your group.

How many years products last		How many years rubbish lasts	
	years		*years*
fridge	15		
audio cassette		aluminium can	
freezer		leather footwear	
sweater		nuclear waste	
telephone		orange peel	
television		plastic bag	
violin		plastic jar / bottle	
white lines on road		wool socks	

PROGRESS TEST 1
Units 1–3

❶ Interest through stress (12 marks)

Underline which of the words in *italics* that would naturally have the most stress.

A Hello, how *are things*¹?

B Great thanks. It's good to *see you*² again. So *what have*³ you been up to?

A Actually, *I've just*⁴ been promoted to *Marketing Manager*⁵.

B Really? That's *fantastic news*⁶, congratulations! *Shall we*⁷ have a drink some time to celebrate?

A *What about*⁸ tomorrow night?

B I think *Friday night*⁹ would suit me better. If that's all right *with you*¹⁰.

A Yes, *that's fine*¹¹. OK, *see you*¹² then.

❷ Meaning through stress (4 marks)

Underline the word in the sentence in *italics* which would be stressed in order to give the meaning below it.

1 *So you have been to Paris.*
  I was under the impression that you hadn't been there.

2 *So she went without Paul.*
  I thought they were going together.

3 *So you think she should come.*
  I thought you said it wasn't a good idea.

4 *So he actually enjoys working for her.*
  I thought he would hate it.

❸ Definitions (10 marks)

Decide whether the definitions for the words below are correct, and rewrite any that are incorrect in the space below.

1 *annual turnover*	amount of sales of goods or services by a company
2 *corporate strategy*	future plans and tactics of a company
3 *joint venture*	permanent collaboration between two companies
4 *net revenue*	money received before taxes have been paid
5 *overseas aid*	foreign investment
6 *power distance*	the extent to which subordinates are consulted by their superiors
7 *retail trade*	businesses selling small quantities of goods to the general public
8 *spin-off*	an unexpected side effect
9 *SWOT analysis*	a method of analysing success, well-being, objectives, and timing
10 *trade union*	a common market for a group of countries

....

....

....

....

❹ Past simple vs present perfect vs present perfect continuous (15 marks)

> ### PROJECT MANAGER
> #### Language Engineering
>
> A position is available as Project Manager for a leading Language Engineering firm located in Berlin. Experience with European Community projects an advantage. Fluent English essential, plus working knowledge of at least two other major European languages. Send CV plus accompanying letter to the Human Resources Manager at

Read the reply to this advertisement on the next page, and put the verbs in brackets into the correct form.

For the attention of the Human
Resources Manager

I am writing with regard to the post you (advertise)
........¹ in the *Times* on March 10. I (graduate)
........² in Linguistics at the University of Bonn in
1995 and (obtain) ....³ a Masters in Applied
Linguistics the following year. Since then I (work)
........⁴ for two different companies. I (work)
........⁵ for Meta 4 in London from 1996 to 1998
and I (begin) ....⁶ my current employment at
TriLogos PLC in 1999.

So far at TriLogus I (complete) ....⁷ three
different applications for EC projects (EAGLES,
PAROLE, RELATOR), and I am currently working on
a natural language system for vending machines
which I (develop) ....⁸ for the last two months.
Over the last three years I (also gain) ....⁹
considerable experience in other aspects of
language engineering as I (attend) ....¹⁰ various
congresses on such areas as artificial intelligence,
language engineering standards, and logic
programming. I (also give) ....¹¹ a series of
workshops on these subjects here at TriLogus, the
last of which will be held at the end of this month.

My native language is Swedish, but I also speak
fluent German as I (take) ....¹² my degree at a
German university. I (travel) ....¹³ widely
throughout Europe, so English is basically my second
language, and I recently (attend) ....¹⁴ a French
course where I (reach) ....¹⁵ an upper
intermediate level. I hope to reach an even higher
level by the end of the current semester.

I look forward to hearing from you in the near
future.

❺ Pronunciation (4 marks)

Underline the <u>one</u> word in each group which
in standard English does not contain the
vowel sound:

1	/ɜ:/ as in *were*	perfect, heard, further, word, first, compare, workshop
2	/eə/ as in *where*	fair, software, venture, sportswear, airport, aftercare, square
3	/ɔ:/ as in *wore*	ensure, backdoor, furthermore, brochure, storage, former, poor
4	/eɪ/ as in *way*	stage, image, freight, buffet, weight, brainstorm, location

❻ Second and third conditionals (10 marks)

Put the verbs in brackets into the correct
conditional form.

e.g. If I *studied* more I *would* probably *pass*
the exam next June.

If I had *studied* more I *would* probably
have passed the exam last June.

1 We ran out of time at the meeting. If we
(have) .... more time, we (cover) ....
all the items on the agenda.

2 She seems reluctant to take on the extra
responsibility. Perhaps if we (give) ....
her a rise in salary, she (accept) ....

3 If I (be) .... in charge of this project,
I (delegate) .... a little more than our
current manager does.

4 Do you think you (take) .... on all this

new work if you (know) .... how much of your time it was going to take up?

5   I'm really sorry. I (tell) .... you earlier if I (have)......... the chance, but I've been busy all day.

❼ Telephoning (15 marks)

Underline the most appropriate word or phrase.

Switchboard British Motors. Good morning. Can I help you?

Kurzhals *I am / This is*¹ Anneliese Kurzhals calling from Metafora PLC.

Switchboard Sorry I didn't *catch / understand*² your name.

Kurzhals Anneliese Kurzhals. Could you *pass me / put me through*³ to Mr John Dean please?

Switchboard Yes, *keep / hold*⁴ the line please. *(pause)* I'm afraid the line is *busy / occupied*⁵ at the moment. *(pause)* Oh, it's free now.

Dean Hello, Production.

Kurzhals Could I *talk / speak*⁶ to John Dean please?

Dean *I am John Dean / Speaking*⁷.

Kurzhals Hello John, *it's / I am*⁸ Anneliese Kurzhals.

Dean Oh Anneliese, I didn't recognise your voice. How *are you doing / do you do*⁹?

Kurzhals *Fine / Well*¹⁰ thanks and you? How's your new *job / work*¹¹ going?

Dean Well, it only started last week, but it's going very *fine / well*¹² thanks.

Kurzhals *Listen / Listen to me*¹³, John, we need to fix a date for the meeting. What about Thursday at nine?

Dean That sounds fine. *We see each other / See you*¹⁴ on Thursday then.

Kurzhals *That's really extremely kind of you / Thanks*¹⁵ John, be seeing you.

❽ Meetings phrases (10 marks)

Insert the phrases in the box into the correct spaces of the mini dialogues.

a	if I just summarized
b	if I've understood you correctly
c	precisely!
d	quite agree
e	shall we move onto the next point
f	so what you're saying
g	sorry, if I could just interrupt you
h	sorry, just one more thing
i	what are your views
j	what I really meant

A .... ¹ on this, Liz?

B Well I think it's time we started making decisions bottom-up.

A .... ² is that decisions should be made at lower levels than now.

B .... ³

C Yes, I .... ⁴ with Liz. I think …

D .... ⁵, I think we're losing track of the main subject here.

A .... ⁶ ? I think we've covered that one now.

B .... ⁷ before we discuss the next item. ....⁸ Liz, what you're suggesting is that we give the people on the shop floor more decision-making power.

A Well, ... ⁹ was that it's the people nearer the bottom, for example the sales staff, who are much closer to the customers. Perhaps it would be best ....¹⁰ what I was saying earlier. So …

9 Small talk (10 marks)

Underline any mistakes that you find and correct them. The host and guest have never met before.

Host How do you do?

Guest *I've got a bit of a cold actually.* [1]

....

Host Come in, take a seat.

Guest *That really is extremely kind of you.* [2]

....

Host Can I get you something to drink - a coffee, some tea?

Guest *No.* [3] ....

Host Do you mind if I smoke?

Guest *Yes I do.* [4] ....

Host Is this the first time you have been here?

Guest *Yes it is, and I feel very honoured to have this opportunity to visit your most illustrious country.* [5]

....

Host And you're the new marketing manager, aren't you?

Guest Yes that's right. I see that you collect butterflies.

Host Yes, I've been collecting them for 40 years.

Guest *Wow!* [6] .... And are those your children in the photo?

Host Yes, the little boy's called Adrian and the girl is Anna.

Guest *Really?* [7] ....

At the end of the meeting …

Host Well, we seem to have covered everything. I'll send you the final contract in the post. (pause) Can I get you a taxi?

Guest *I'll walk.* [8] ....

Host Well, it was a great pleasure meeting you.

Guest *You're welcome.* [9] ....

Host And I hope we'll be able to meet again soon.

Guest *So long.* [10] ....

Host Goodbye, and thank you for coming.

10 Culture (10 marks)

Decide whether the following statements are true or false.

1 Most English people wouldn't mind you criticizing their royal family. ☐

2 Australian business people tend to dress more informally than Americans. ☐

3 In Japan business cards are exchanged with both hands. ☐

4 People tend to use first names in most English speaking countries. ☐

5 Work titles are generally used when talking to business colleagues in most mid- and southern European countries. ☐

6 In China, the most senior person generally enters the meeting room last. ☐

7 At meetings in Australia it is acceptable to ask people what position they hold when their role at the meeting is not clear. ☐

8 In the USA business people take punctuality more seriously than their Arab counterparts. ☐

9 The Republic of Ireland is part of the United Kingdom. ☐

10 The Chinese say their surname before their first name. ☐

PROGRESS TEST 2
Units 4–6

❶ Numbers (5 marks)

Write the numbers and dates as words.

1 0.55 ....
2 2:1 ....
3 15 x 40 ....
4 (phone) 980–4467 ....
5 (date) 10.03.2009 ....

❷ Countable and uncountable nouns (10 marks)

1 Five of these words can be made plural. Find them and give the plural forms.

advice	feedback	information
baggage	furniture	knowhow
currency	gold	profit
expertise	hardware	progress
evidence	help	proposal
explanation	homework	suggestion

....

....

....

....

....

2 Write the plurals of these words:

analysis ....

criterion ....

formula ....

knife ....

series ....

❸ Definitions (10 marks)

Decide whether the definitions for the words below are correct, and rewrite any that are incorrect in the space below.

1 *advise*   give suggestions
2 *briefcase*   short legal proceedings
3 *delegation*   a group of representatives
4 *disconcerting*   upsetting, embarrassing, confusing
5 *erroneous*   convenient
6 *exhaust (n)*   discharge from engine
7 *hint*   recommend
8 *infringement*   failure to observe terms or conditions
9 *roughly*   slightly
10 *sympathetic*   nice

....

....

....

....

....

❹ Phrasal verbs (5 marks)

Match the verbs with their definitions.

branch out	diversify
bring up	leave
check in	occur
come up	propose
drop off	register

❺ A letter home (10 marks)

Underline the correct alternatives below.

Dear Jim

This is a just a quick note to let you know how things are working out on my *trip / travel*[1]. The *journey / travel*[2] here was a nightmare – over 24 hours. When we finally *landed / took off*[3] I went to the car *hiring / rental*[4] desk. They had no reservation in my name so the *travel / travels*[5] agency must have made a mistake somewhere. Then I realized I'd left my driving *licence / patent / permission*[6] at home. Luckily I managed to get Susy to fax it to me, and I set off down the highway. Then I forgot to turn *off / out*[7] at the second junction, then I ... well, I won't bore you with any of the other details. One of the first things I noticed is that the cost of living has *raised / risen*[8] considerably since I was last here. They've *raised / risen*[9] the prices in the hotels by about 20%, and the new prices didn't even *comprehend / include*[10] breakfast. But as far as the actual business is

❻ Future simple vs future continuous (10 marks)

Underline the most appropriate form.

1   I will *give / be giving* you lift. I will *go / be going* past the airport anyway on my way home.

2   Oh no, the car will not *start / be starting*. I will *have / be having* to call the garage.

3   I will just *wrap / be wrapping* this up for you madam. Will you *pay / be paying* by cash or credit card?

4   Will you just *come / be coming* to my office a second Ms Brown? Yes of course, I will *be / be being* with you straight away.

5   She's got masses of work so she will not *come / be coming* till next week, but I will *see / be seeing* if she can make it earlier in the week than later.

❼ Reported speech (20 marks)

Put the sentences into reported speech using the prompts in brackets.

e.g. Don't forget to post the letter. (She / remind / me)

She reminded me to post the letter.

1   Will you please reconsider? (I / urge / them)

....

2   We must have it immediately. (We / insist)

....

3   I'll do it as soon as I can. (I / say)

....

4   Would you like a drink? (He / ask / her)

....

5   Don't worry! It will never happen. (They / assure / me)

....

6   Ring me when you've finished. (She / tell / him)

....

7   Really, I had no other choice. (I / explain)

....

8   Why don't you go by plane? (I / suggest / they)

....

9 You should go there before 8.00 p.m.
   (They / recommend / we)

   ....

10 I promise I didn't touch it. (He / deny)

   ....

❽ The definite article (10 marks)

Insert the definite article where appropriate.

1 .... Table 1 shows .... figures for last year.

2 We can meet outside .... school on Dean Street but I've got to go to .... bank first.

3 Have you ever been to .... Great Britain? No, but I've been to .... Republic of Ireland.

4 What time is .... dinner with .... Chinese customers?

5 What do you normally have for .... lunch? I usually have .... pasta.

❾ Prepositions (5 marks)

Insert the correct preposition.

1 VAT has gone up slightly .... 20%; before it was 19%.

2 The cost of living has risen .... 2%; it was 3% now it's 5%.

3 We can only justify an increase .... $25 per unit.

4 The increase .... overhead costs can easily be offset.

5 Inflation now stands .... 3%.

❿ Telephoning (15 marks)

Insert one appropriate word in each space.

Secretary I'm ....[1] but she's not in her office. She should be back ....[2] about half an hour.

Caller 1 Could you ask her to ring me ....[3] ?

Secretary Do you think you could speak ....[4] a little, please? The ....[5] is really bad.

Caller 1 Yes, could you ask her to call me ....[6] 050–273734, before seven tonight. If not I'll try again ....[7] Thursday morning.

— —

Secretary I'm afraid she's held ....[8] at a meeting.

Caller 2 Sorry, what did you ....[9] ?

Secretary She's ....[10] a meeting at the moment. Would you like ....[11] to take a message?

Caller 2 Yes, could you ask her to send me the new catalogue? The address is Nicole Schulze. That's S–C–H–U–L–Z–E, Von Melle Park, that's three ....[12] , von V–O–N …

Secretary Sorry, could you speak a ....[13] more slowly please?

Caller 2 Yes of course. Von Melle Park: V–O–N–M–E–L–L–E Park number 6.

Secretary E–L–L–E, OK. I've got ....[14]. I'll ....[15] her as soon as she comes back.

© Oxford University Press **PHOTOCOPIABLE**

PROGRESS TEST 3
Units 7–9

❶ Pronunciation (20 marks; 5 for each section)

1   Underline the five words that have two syllables.

added	filed
answered	gauged
asked	measured
dated	passed
experienced	queried

2   Underline the pairs of words that are not pronounced in exactly the same way.

hole / whole
right / write
vile / while
wear / where
wood / would

3   Underline the five words in which *th* is pronounced /θ/ as in *thank*.

length	these	through
method	they	together
otherwise	this	whether
than	three	with
there	though	withhold

4   Underline the five words that have the same pronunciation as a noun or a verb.

exploit	produce	reject
feature	project	support
graduate	record	target
object	recruit	welcome

❷ Definitions (10 marks)

Decide whether the definitions for the words below are correct, and rewrite any that are incorrect in the space below.

1	*anticipate*	to expect
2	*benchmark*	standard for measuring quality
3	*canvass*	to examine in detail, solicit
4	*feasibility*	level of comprehensiveness
5	*finalize*	to target
6	*freebie*	kind of device
7	*fuel*	material for providing power
8	*shortcoming*	brief visit
9	*smooth*	opposite of rough
10	*snag*	light lunch

....

....

....

....

....

❸ Phrasal verbs (5 marks)

Match the verbs with their meanings.

1	carry out	a	arrange, resolve, settle
2	give off	b	collect
3	look forward to	c	emit
4	pick up	d	perform
5	sort out	e	think about the future

❹ Sequences (10 marks)

Insert the words and phrases in the box into the gaps in the presentation below.

a	at the end	f	in the end
b	before	g	once
c	finally	h	secondly
d	first	i	subsequently
e	firstly	j	then

Well, thank you all very much for coming along. This morning I'm going to be talking to you about the new shipment process. By the way, I'll be taking questions ....¹ of the presentation, if that's all right with you. Let's just have a look at what I've got planned for this morning. ....², we'll be looking at the new selection scheme. ....³ we have looked at a few examples from the selection procedure we can ....⁴ move on to packaging; and ....⁵ I'm going to review the new shipping requirements for the Middle East market.

But ....⁶ we do that I want to tell you why we're introducing the new shipment process. When the original process was introduced ten years ago we had two main problems: ....⁷ we had to replace a great deal of outdated equipment, and ....⁸ the whole process was very labour-intensive. ....⁹, and after a lot of hard deliberation, we had to take a series of redundancy measures which were ....¹⁰ partially retracted as a result of trade union intervention. The situation today is

❺ Future simple vs future continuous vs future perfect (10 marks)

Underline the correct form. If both forms are possible, underline both.

1   I think that by 2020 they will *discover / have discovered* a new device for learning languages and that people will already *use / be using* it on a regular basis.

2   When you *have / will have finished* that, will you *help / be helping* me with this please?

3   I think I'll *take / be taking* my umbrella because I'm sure it'll *rain / be raining* when I arrive in London.

4   By the time I speak to you next I will *see / have seen* the new equipment, so I will *be / have been* able to tell you all about it.

5   I'll *arrive / be arriving* at 2.00 p.m. Don't worry about food, as I'll already *eat / have eaten*.

❻ *be* vs *have* (5 marks)

Underline the correct form.

1   Taxes *are / have* raised every year.
2   She *is / has* gone to Bejing.
3   The work *is / has* finished.
4   Her English *is / has* improved.
5   The problems *are / have* increased.

❼ The passive (10 marks)

Continue the second sentence so that it means the same as the first sentence.

1   They are making a lot of progress.
    A lot of progress ....

2   They were told to go directly to the hotel.
    Someone ....

3   I will inform her of your decision.
    She ....

4 They don't speak English there.

English ....

5 They would have built an extra one if there had been time.

An extra one ....

❽ Infinitive vs gerund (10 marks)

Underline the correct form

1 *Making / To make* mistakes is easy.

2 The aim of the presentation is *convincing / to convince* them to buy our products.

3 I'd like *seeing / to see* the manager please.

4 I enjoy *watching / to watch* old movies.

5 We look forward to *hearing / hear* from you in the near future.

6 We stopped on our way *looking / to look* at the new theatre.

7 I forgot *telling / to tell* her about the new arrangements.

8 I remember *telling / to tell* her because she reacted quite badly.

9 We stopped *using / to use* faxes a couple of years ago.

10 Will you remember *turning / to turn* off all the lights please?

❾ Making appointments and welcoming visitors (20 marks)

Insert one word into each gap in the three dialogues.

Dialogue 1: A and B are talking on the phone.

A Hello, this is Jo Bean. You ....[1] remember that we met at the congress last week.

B ....[2] to hear you. How are you?

A Fine thanks. I was wondering if we could meet

..............[3] some time at my office. Would a week on Thursday ....[4] you?

B ....[5] me just look at my schedule for that week. I'm afraid I'm going to be ....[6] up all day in various meetings.

A Could you possibly ....[7] the following Wednesday?

B That sounds fine. ....[8] you on Wednesday the tenth then.

A Excellent. I'll get my secretary to fax you details of how to ....[9] here.

Dialogue 2: C goes to meet D at the airport.

C Good to see you. I hope you haven't been waiting ....[10]. ....[11] was your flight?

D The landing was a bit ....[12] but apart from that it was fine.

C Would you like a bite to eat before we ....[13] off?

D No thanks, I ate on the plane.

C ....[14] I help you with your luggage?

D No that's all right, I think I can ....[15].

Dialogue 3: E is a receptionist, F a visitor.

E Would you ....[16] just signing the register?

F OK. *(signs register)* Could you tell me where I can leave all these samples?

E Yes of course, the laboratory is just ....[17] the corridor, last door on the left. But ....[18] the floor, it's just been washed.

E *(F returns)* Ms Smith is ....[19] to see you now. If you ....[20] just follow me, I'll take you to her office.

PROGRESS TEST 4
Units 10–12

❶ Sentence stress (15 marks)

The text below is the beginning of a presentation. Indicate which of the words in italics you would stress by <u>underlining</u> them.

Thank you[1] very much for *coming here*[2] today and for *your interest*[3] in the Meta 4 Corporation and the strong family of brands and businesses that *we represent*[4]. As I am sure *you are aware*[5], Meta 4's heritage brand and *product line*[6] has traditionally been in *home-based appliances*[7]. What you might *not know*[8] is that in the last two years *we have extended*[9] our business and product lines, and *our reach*[10] in the *market place*[11]. All of our businesses are linked through a strategy based on brand strength, robust product design, and dependability, *all of which*[12] are aimed at meeting the needs of home and *commercial appliance owners*[13]. Our pledge to our shareholders, customers, and consumers alike is to *grow profitably*[14] at a faster-than-industry rate through a brand leadership supported by *superior product innovation*[15] and performance.

❷ Definitions (10 marks)

Decide whether the definitions for the words below are correct, and rewrite any that are incorrect in the space below.

1 *cornerstone*   scheduled event in a plan

2 *ensure*   guarantee, make safe

3 *enterprise*   main doorway of a building

4 *gathering*   reunion, meeting

5 *liabilities*   tangible and intangible resources

6 *outline*   brief description

7 *overheads*   spotlights

8 *pamper*   outdated mechanical equipment

9 *recruitment*   staff turnover

10 *yield*   earnings per share

....

....

....

....

....

❸ Food (10 marks)

Decide which of the following are likely to be served in Great Britain as:

a	starters / appetisers
b	main courses
c	desserts

1 baked bananas

2 cheese

3 chicken curry

4 chicken liver paté

5 grilled sirloin steak

6 smoked salmon

7 strawberries

8 warm vegetable salad

9 prawn cocktail

10 roast duck

❹ At the restaurant (10 marks)

Insert an appropriate auxiliary. More than one may be possible.

1 .... you help me read the menu please?

2 .... I ask if they have a vegetarian menu?

3 .... I order for you?

4 .... you order for me please?

5 .... you rather I ordered for you?

6 .... you mind if I smoke?

7 .... we see if they've got any champagne?

8 .... you like some more wine?

9 .... you pass the bread please?

10 .... you bring us the bill please?

❺ Past simple vs past continuous vs past perfect (15 marks)

Put the verbs in brackets into the past simple, continuous, or perfect. Then try to work out the answer! (No marks for guessing correctly; the answer is at the end of the test.)

An egg salesman (get) ....^{1} out of his car in the evening when his little girl (come) ....^{2} up and (ask) ....^{3} him how many eggs he (sell) ....^{4} that day. He (reply) ....^{5}, 'My first customer (say) ....^{6} that he already (buy) ....^{7} his eggs so he not (buy) ....^{8} any. When I (meet) ....^{9} my second customer she (go) ....^{10} out to the supermarket, so I (stop) ....^{11} her and (offer) ....^{12} her my eggs. She said she would buy half my eggs and half an egg more. The third and the fourth customers said the same thing. So at the end of the day I (realize) ....^{13} that I (finish) ....^{14} all my eggs without having to break a single egg all day. How many do you think I (sell) ....^{15}?

The little girl thought for a moment and said, 'Seven!'

❻ Acronyms (5 marks)

Write out in full the following acronyms.

1 CEO ....

2 GDP ....

3 IT ....

4 MD ....

5 VAT ....

❼ Phrasal / prepositional verbs (15 marks)

1 Correct, where necessary, the position of the words in **bold** in the sentences below.

a I don't want to go details **into**.

b I'll be going various issues **over**.

c I'd like to put some new ideas **forward**.

d I'll just switch the video **on**.

e We are looking it **into**.

2 Match the phrasal / prepositional verb with its meaning.

leave out	allocate
run through	conclude
set aside	gain control
take over	omit
wind up	quickly check

3 Replace the verbs in italics with an equivalent verb from the box below plus a preposition or adverb.

carry	~~go~~	look	put	set	think

e.g. We'll have to *examine* it later. <u>go over</u>

a They've just *established* a new branch in Barcelona. ....

b   The meeting has been *postponed* until next Wednesday. ....

c   I've been *considering* what you said and I'm afraid the answer is still 'no'. ....

d   She's *performed* the various changes we asked for. ....

e   We can't guarantee anything but we'll certainly *investigate* the matter. ....

❽ Modal verbs (10 marks)

Underline the correct form.

1   You *have to / must* come and see us when you're next in town.

2   You *don't have to / mustn't* do it now; it can wait until later.

3   We *had to spend / should have spent* more than we were expecting, but we're happy with the result.

4   The meeting *had / was supposed* to start at 10.00, but by 10.30 only half the people had arrived.

5   We *should have tried / were supposed to try* to get them to lower the price. Then we would have got a better deal.

6   You *have to / should* try doing it the other way round; you might find it works better.

7   You *shouldn't have done / didn't have to do* it without asking my permission.

8   *Can / May* you help me to shift this computer into the next room?

9   *I can / may* be late for the meeting; if I am please start without me.

10 She *can / may* speak six different languages – she's a genius!

❾ Permission (10 marks)

Continue the second sentence so that it means the same as the first.

1   We weren't allowed to go in.

    They didn't allow ....

2   You can have it for $100.

    I'll let ....

3   They didn't permit her to cross the border.

    She ....

4   This program allows you to work much faster.

    You can ....

5   If you move it there you'll be able to see it better.

    Moving it there will enable ....

Answer to exercise 6: The first customer didn't buy any eggs. The second bought four, the third two, the fourth one. (This is the only solution that leaves him without any broken eggs.)

PROGRESS TEST 5
Units 13–14

❶ Pronunciation and stress (10 marks)

1 List the following words according to the sound they contain.

Asian	Greenwich	scenario
Leicester	scene	Yorkshire
chance	Manchester	sceptical
Chicago	pleasure	science
sure	brochure	vision

/s/ as in *song* ....

/ʃ/ as in *ship* ....

/ʒ/ as in *leisure* ....

/tʃ/ as in *church* ....

2 Underline the five words that in English have the stress on the first syllable.

Alaska	Japan	New Delhi
Beijing	Manchester	Oxford
Brazil	Manhattan	Paris
Canterbury	Milan	Stockholm

❷ Vocabulary (10 marks)

Decide whether the definitions for the words below are correct, and rewrite any that are incorrect in the space below.

1 *boom*	a sharp rise in price in the stock market
2 *cash flow*	pattern of receipts and expenditure
3 *deficit*	excess of income over expenditure
4 *infrastructure*	underlying foundation
5 *overtime*	system allowing employees choice in working schedule
6 *patent*	driving licence
7 *retirement*	withdrawal of money from bank account
8 *safeguard*	precaution or protective measure
9 *subsidy*	a grant of money
10 *surplus*	in excess of the prescribed limit

❸ Concessions and conditions (10 marks)

Underline the correct forms.

1 If I *will have / have / would have / had* any problems I *will / would* let you know.

2 *Even though / if we* reduced our price they were still not interested.

3 At this point *if / whether* they come or not it's not going to make much difference.

4 Perhaps if you *mentioned / had mentioned* the licensing terms at the beginning they *would be / have been* more amenable, but as it turned out it didn't make any difference.

5 I think we *do / will do* it now, *unless you / if you don't* prefer to do it tomorrow.

6 If you *made / had made* the arrangements properly for the hotel we wouldn't be in this mess now – so where are we going to sleep?

7 If you work hard in this company they generally *give / will give / would give* you a bonus at the end of the year.

❹ Pre-negotiation tactics (15 marks)

A sales manager is preparing for an important negotiation. Complete the memo below from the manager to her assistant, using the phrases below.

I'd like to clarify our position before our meeting in Bejing next week. As we understand it their current ....¹ is $4,800 per package, though their original ....² was for $5,000. I think the most we should be ....³ should be $4,600, considering that we might be placing an order, more than 10% up on last year. I know that Mr Lo will ....⁴, and he's unlikely to accept our offer, so we need a few ....⁵. We could:

• ....⁶ to our warehouse.
• ....⁷ the insurance and import duties.
• pay ....⁸ after 60 rather than 90 days.

In return I think they could speed up their ....⁹ and we could ask them to improve their after-sales service by setting up a telephone ....¹⁰.

I insist that we stick to the $4,600, otherwise ....¹¹ are going to be too tight. However, it's important to achieve a win-win agreement, so I'd like you to think of a few more ....¹² so that we can find a ....¹³. We've only got a couple of days in Beijing, so the last thing I want is some kind of ....¹⁴ where neither side is prepared to compromise.

I'm fairly tied up over the next couple of days, so I suggest we ....¹⁵ on the plane.

a happy medium
b asking price
c delivery times
d hotline
e strike a hard bargain
f cover

g quotation
h hammer out the details
i stalemate situation
j our margins
k pay for transport
l their invoices
m fall back options
n tradeables
o willing to offer

❺ Prepositions and adverbs (10 marks)
Underline the correct word.

1 Can you check *in / out* their prices for me?
2 We're trying to break *into / onto* a new market.
3 We're faced *of / with* a problem here.
4 You could try shopping *about / around* for a better deal.
5 She's going to send *off / out* for details.
6 We couldn't agree *on / with* a price.
7 They've been haggling *over / under* the terms all day.
8 Let's hammer *in / out* the details, shall we?
9 We're going to keep that tactic *in / on* reserve.
10 We could take that *for / in* part exchange.

❻ At a trade fair (10 marks)

Below is an extract from a conversation at a trade fair. Number the sentences in the order that they would have been said.

a Both, really. I wasn't aware that it would make any difference. ......
b Can I ask what you do exactly? Are you in men's or women's fashions? ......
c Fine. I should be back in my office on the 13th so I'll expect a call shortly after then. ......

d I see you've been at our stand for quite a while. Is there any specific piece of equipment you're interested in? ......

e No problem. Perhaps if you could leave me your card I'll get one of our salespeople to contact you. ......

f That'd be great. Thank you. *(later)* Yes, well I have to say I'm quite impressed. ......

g Well, first I'd like to know whether it would be possible for someone to visit our company. ......

h Well, I'm looking for some new ways to machine sleeves onto jackets. ......

i Well, this machine over here actually makes a different sewing pattern depending on the material being used – silk for example is more common on women's clothes than on men's. Would you like me to give you a demonstration? ......

j Would you be interested in a quotation? We could certainly make you an interesting offer. ......

❼ Problem time (20 marks)

Fill the gaps with the appropriate form of the verb in brackets.

e.g. Please inform us as soon as possible, as next week we <u>will be closing</u> our books for this year. (close)

1 As this is not the first time this .... we would be grateful for immediate action. (happen)

2 Could you also let us .... exactly when you are planning to release an updated version. (know)

3 I think you'll find that in the maintenance agreement this kind of repair is not .... (cover)

4 I'm extremely sorry about this, I .... with the accounts department immediately. (check)

5 While checking our credit card statement we discovered that we have been .... for twenty items, whereas the shipment form clearly states that we ordered and received ten items. (charge)

6 The contract was .... to be signed by all members of the Board of Directors, not just one of them. (mean)

7 There must have .... a mistake on the shipment form. I'll look into it. (be)

8 There is still no sign of lot #434 despite .... advice of shipment from you more than two weeks ago. (receive)

9 When we spoke on Monday, you said that you .... them off on Tuesday, but there's still no sign of them. (send)

10 Where are the goods? We .... delivery last week. (expect)

© Oxford University Press

❽ *do* and *make* (15 marks)

Insert *do* or *make* into the spaces using either the present perfect (active or passive), present perfect continuous or past simple (active or passive). Change the word order where necessary.

A How long you ....[1] your current job?

B Well, actually, I only ....[2] manager last year. They ....[3] me an offer I just couldn't refuse.

A (You) ....[4] any business abroad?

B I ....[5] three trips to China so far, to a shoe factory in Bejing. I ....[6] a terrible mistake on the first day, I mistook a technician for the MD.

A (This factory) ....[7] shoes for long?

B For about 30 years. Until not all that long ago most of the shoes ....[8] by hand.

A (And you) ....[9] any suggestions to them on how to improve productivity?

B Yes, and I think we ....[10] a lot of progress, productivity has already gone up by half of our target in just over a year.

PROGRESS TESTS
Answer Key

Test 1

❶
1 things
2 see
3 what
4 just
5 Marketing
6 fantastic
7 shall
8 what
9 Friday
10 you
11 fine
12 see

❷
1 have
2 without
3 should
4 enjoys

❸
1 correct
2 correct
3 temporary collaboration
4 after taxes
5 help to foreign countries
6 correct
7 correct
8 subsidiary or new company coming out of original company
9 strengths, weaknesses, opportunities, threats
10 labour union

❹
1 advertised
2 graduated
3 obtained
4 have worked
5 worked
6 began
7 have completed
8 have been developing
9 have also gained
10 have attended
11 have also been giving
12 took
13 have travelled
14 attended
15 reached

❺
1 compare
2 venture
3 brochure
4 image

❻
1 had had, would have covered
2 gave, would accept
3 were / was, would delegate
4 would have taken, had known
5 would have told, had had

❼
1 This is
2 catch
3 put me through
4 hold
5 busy
6 speak
7 speaking
8 it's
9 are you doing
10 Fine
11 job
12 well
13 Listen
14 See you
15 Thanks

❽
1 i
2 f
3 c
4 d
5 g
6 e
7 h
8 b
9 j
10 a

❾
1 How do you do? / Pleased to meet you.
2 Thank you.
3 No, thanks, I've just had some. / I won't at the moment thanks. (or similar)
4 No, not at all. / Well, I'd rather you didn't.
5 Yes, it is.
6 Really? / How interesting. (or similar)
7 They're lovely. (or similar)
8 Thank you, but I think I'll walk. I'd like to see the city. (or similar)
9 And you too.
10 Goodbye. (or similar)

❿
1 F
2 T
3 T
4 T
5 T
6 F (first)
7 T
8 T
9 F
10 T

Test 2

❶
1 zero / nought point five five
2 two to one
3 fifteen times forty
4 nine eight oh / zero double four (four four) six seven
5 March (the) tenth two thousand and nine

2
1 currencies, explanations, profits, proposals, suggestions
2 analyses, criteria, formulae, knives, series

3
1 correct
2 case for business documents
3 correct
4 correct
5 wrong
6 correct
7 suggest indirectly
8 correct
9 approximately
10 understanding of, in agreement with

4
branch out – diversify
bring up – propose
check in – register
come up – occur
drop off – leave

5
1 trip
2 journey
3 landed
4 rental
5 travel
6 licence
7 off
8 risen
9 raised
10 include

6
1 give, be going
2 start, have
3 wrap, be paying
4 come, be
5 be coming, see

7
1 I urged them to reconsider.
2 We insisted that we (must) have it immediately.

3 I said I would do it as soon as I could.
4 He asked her if she would like a drink.
5 They assured me that it would never happen.
6 She told him to ring her when he had finished.
7 I explained that (really) I had no other choice.
8 I suggested that they (should) go by plane.
9 They recommended that we (should) go there before 8.00.
10 He denied that he had touched it / He denied touching it.

8
1 – , the
2 the, the
3 –, the
4 the, the
5 –, –

9
1 to
2 by
3 of
4 in
5 at

10
1 sorry
2 in
3 back
4 up
5 line
6 on
7 on
8 up
9 say
10 in
11 me
12 words
13 bit / little
14 that / it
15 tell

Test 3

1
1 added, answered, dated, measured, queried
2 vile, while
3 length, method, three, through, withhold
4 feature, recruit, support, target, welcome

2
1 correct
2 correct
3 correct
4 capability and practicality of use
5 make final, bring to completion
6 something given free, complimentary gift
7 correct
8 deficiency, disadvantage
9 correct
10 drawback

3
1 d
2 c
3 e
4 b
5 a

4
1 a
2 d / e
3 g
4 j
5 c
6 b
7 e / d
8 h
9 f
10 i

5
1 have discovered, be using
2 have, help
3 take, be raining
4 have seen, be
5 be arriving, have eaten

6
1 are
2 has
3 is
4 has
5 have

7
1 is being made
2 told them to go directly to the hotel
3 will be informed of your decision
4 is not spoken there
5 would have been built if there had been time

8
1 making
2 to convince
3 to see
4 watching
5 hearing
6 to look
7 to tell
8 telling
9 using
10 to turn

9
1 may
2 great / good / nice
3 up
4 suit
5 let
6 tied
7 come
8 see
9 get
10 long
11 how
12 bumpy / rough
13 set
14 can / may
15 manage
16 mind
17 down / along
18 mind
19 ready
20 will / would

Test 4

1
1 Thank
2 coming
3 interest
4 represent
5 aware
6 product
7 home
8 not
9 extended
10 reach
11 market
12 all
13 commercial
14 grow
15 product

2
1 foundation
2 correct
3 company, business project
4 correct
5 money owed by a company
6 correct
7 regular costs of running a business
8 treat with excessive kindness
9 process of taking on new staff
10 correct

3
1 c
2 c
3 b
4 a
5 b
6 a (b is also acceptable)
7 c
8 b (a is also acceptable)
9 a
10 b

4
1 can / could / would
2 shall
3 shall / can / may
4 could / can / would / will
5 would
6 do
7 shall
8 would
9 will / could / can
10 would / will / could

5
1 was getting
2 came
3 asked
4 had sold
5 replied
6 said
7 had already bought
8 didn't buy
9 met
10 was going
11 stopped
12 offered
13 realized
14 had finished
15 sold

6
1 Chief Executive Officer
2 Gross Domestic Product
3 Information Technology
4 Managing Director
5 Value Added Tax

7
1 a go into details
b going over various issues
c correct ('put forward some new ideas' is also correct).
d correct ('switch on the video' is also correct).
e looking into it
2 leave out – omit
run through – quickly check
set aside – allocate
take over – gain control
wind up – conclude
3 a set up
b put off
c thinking over
d carried out
e look into

8
1 must
2 don't have to
3 had to spend
4 was supposed
5 should have tried
6 should
7 shouldn't have done
8 can
9 may
10 can

9
1 They didn't allow us to go in.
2 I'll let you have it for $100.
3 She wasn't permitted to cross the border.
4 You can work much faster with this program.
5 Moving it there will enable you to see it better.

Test 5

Give ¹/₂ mark for each correct answer.

1
1 /s/ Leicester, scenario, scene, sceptical, science
/ʃ/ brochure, Chicago, sure, Yorkshire
/ʒ/ Asian, pleasure, vision
/tʃ/ chance, Manchester, Greenwich
2 Canterbury, Manchester, Oxford, Paris, Stockholm

2
1 period of business prosperity, industrial expansion
2 correct
3 excess of expenditure over income
4 correct
5 hours worked over the standard limit

6 exclusive right to produce something
7 stopping work because you have reached the age limit
8 correct
9 correct
10 profit, beyond requirements

3
1 have, will
2 though
3 whether
4 had mentioned, have been
5 will do, unless you
6 had made
7 give

4
1 b
2 g
3 o
4 e
5 m
6 k
7 f
8 l
9 c
10 d
11 j
12 n
13 a
14 i
15 h

5
1 out
2 into
3 with
4 around
5 off
6 on
7 over
8 out
9 in
10 in

6
Deduct one mark for any sentence out of order.
1 d
2 h
3 b
4 a
5 i
6 f
7 j
8 g
9 e
10 c

7
1 has happened
2 know
3 covered
4 will check
5 charged
6 meant
7 been
8 having received
9 were going to send / would send / would be sending
10 were expecting / expected

8
Give 1 mark for using the correct tense, ¹/₂ a mark for correct use of *do* and *make*. (i.e. 1 ¹/₂ for each question.
1 have you been doing
2 was only made
3 made
4 have you done / have you been doing
5 have made
6 made
7 has this factory been making
8 were made
9 have you made
10 have been making / have made